WHO'S GOT GOD?

JEREMY SEELY & JORDAN ADAMS

Who's Got God?
Copyright © 2011 by Jeremy Seely and Jordan Adams
All rights reserved.

ISBN 978-0-578-08256-1

Cover Design: Monica Seely

Cover images: © Drizzd | Dreamstime.com
              © Tombaky | Dreamstime.com

First Edition

Jermo Productions
Irvine, CA

For Monica

And for Jake, may you grow to become a Mighty Man of God

For Corinne

And for Hailey

FOREWORD

In a world where the norm is filled with argument and debate, primarily driven by the desire to be right, many times civility and tolerance are the missing ingredients. Political correctness, propaganda and positioning fill up the religious air-waves so that it's impossible to feel you can know the truth about anything. *Who's Got God?* is a breath of fresh air, using the best communication channel possible—authentic conversation filled with respect and keeping one another's integrity intact. This is not propaganda or preaching, but a pure experience of true persuasion.

I have had the privilege of observing this conversation unfold over the years. When I first read an interaction between Jeremy and Jordan, there was no doubt that this was an interesting conversation, even compelling! It's rare that a conversation such as this can be recorded and now shared with those who have ears to hear and eyes to see. It's even rarer that a conversation such as this can be packaged to be helpful to so many. May this conversation serve as a catalyst to advance many more conversations that will bring a greater sense of reality to your own faith, however you describe it.

Tim Timmons
Blogger & Mentor

ACKNOWLEDGEMENTS

To my wife Monica, whose ideas and hard work were the catalyst and the engineering for the creation of this book. It would not have been done without you.

To my writing partner-in-crime Jordan Adams. His passion for peace and increased love in the world has been inspiring and uplifting. If more Christians possessed Jordan's heart this book would not be needed. Although we disagree mightily on several core issues, you have taught me greatly in this area, and I am only sorry I did not express this more in our writings.

To my mentor Tim Timmons, who taught me how to challenge "Churchiantiy" while still loving Jesus with all your heart, soul, mind, and strength (and is the source of many of my stories).

To my mother, who has both taught and exemplified the unconditional love of Jesus, and has been the biggest spiritual influence on my life.

Finally to Jesus, who teaches me how to be a better man every day and gives overwhelming grace without favor to all who ask.

To my wife Corinne for her unending patience, guidance and love.

To my daughter Hailey who reminds me how to be joyous, curious, spontaneous and human on a daily basis.

To my Mum Carol Adams who has spent a life time supporting me in every way there is to support a person. Her unflinching love has been an anchor in times both high and low.

And to my favorite mentor Stephen Chandler. The truth in his work encourages, challenges, uplifts and inspires.

A special thanks to my Brother Jeres (Jeremy). This has been a wonderful experience! I am awed and inspired by his peaceful heart and spirit.

PREFACE

Two friends, two faiths, and a joke about a famous radio psychologist... that's how it all got started. In the summer of 2000, Jeremy Seely & Jordan Adams were working as actors together at a murder mystery dinner theatre in Southern California (thus why you'll see them refer to each other by some strange names--their character names--at times). When Jordan sent off one of those ubiquitous forwarded email jokes to his colleagues, he had no idea that he was writing the first words of a 2-year long conversation - one that would drive two friends to reexamine and challenge their most fundamental beliefs.

This book, *Who's Got God?*, can be viewed in two ways. On one level, it is a thorough layman's introduction into the beliefs and defense of both New Thought and Christian philosophy. Mr. Adams' spiritual beliefs fall within the expansive ideals of the New Thought movement, while Mr. Seely defines himself as a follower of Jesus and non-denominational Christian. The 'surface' purpose of this book, and the prototypical emails that make it up, is to convince the other that their beliefs are the 'true' beliefs that should be followed.

On a different level, however, the book reveals another, more vital purpose running underneath. *Who's Got God?* ends up being a book about tolerance. And not just a flimsy, wishy-washy kind that says "every belief is the same and it's all okay with me," but a real, true, capital 'T' kind of tolerance. The two authors discovered, quite by accident, that when differences are treated with respect and are really heard, common ground can be found much more often than expected. Imagine the good and constructive work that could be accomplished around the world if large numbers of people could disagree with dignity, while focusing on common goals and retaining a sense of spiritual brotherhood and sisterhood!

We think *Who's Got God?* represents a step in that direction. It is a template for discussing our differences. It shows how one can be open-minded to opposing ideas, see the truth in the other side and even give ground when needed, all without feeling that one's own cherished ideas are being overthrown in the process. Certainly there is nothing new or noteworthy about this attitude; it may have been forgotten or misplaced in recent times, but never destroyed. There always have and always will be those individuals, however much in the minority they may be, who practice this ability; the authors' hope is to extend it to many more thousands across the country.

Not only are Americans forgetting the concept of tolerance today, but far too many also live their lives with unexamined spiritual beliefs. Whether we've been too busy or just plain lazy, too many don't know why they believe what they (profess to) believe. These beliefs are often based on personal feelings or traditions, but hardly ever on sound reasons that have been carefully researched and meditated on. The other hope we have for this book is that readers will examine their own lives and come to a greater understanding of their own faith.

In the process of trying to "convert" each other, we discovered that we shared more in common than we thought, and found a deep appreciation even in our differences. We believe people on both sides of the issue can review the case made by each and decide for themselves who presents the better one. Many readers may discover their own spirituality for the first time; others will rediscover long-buried religious feelings, and still others will be persuaded to the truth of one or the other worldview.

Where will you end up? Well, God only knows…

From: Jordan Adams <jadams@_____.net>
To: Jeremy Seely <jseely@_____.com>
Sent: Tuesday, June 6, 2000
Subject: Fwd: God's Law

Dear Dr. Laura,

Thank you for doing so much to educate people regarding God's law. I have learned a great deal from you, and I try to share that knowledge with as many people as I can.

When someone tries to defend the homosexual lifestyle, for example, I simply remind him that Leviticus 18:22 clearly states it to be an abomination. End of debate. I do need some advice from you, however, regarding some of the specific laws and how to best follow them.

When I burn a bull on the altar as a sacrifice, I know it creates a pleasing odor for the Lord (Lev. 1:9). The problem is my neighbors. They claim the odor is not pleasing to them. How should I deal with this?

I would like to sell my daughter into slavery, as it suggests in Exodus 21:7. In this day and age, what do you think would be a fair price for her?

I know that I am allowed no contact with a woman while she is in her period of menstrual uncleanliness (Lev. 15:19-24). The problem is, how do I tell? I have tried asking, but most women take offense.

Lev. 25:44 states that I may buy slaves from the nations that are around us. A friend of mine claims that this applies to Mexicans but not Canadians. Can you clarify?

I have a neighbor who insists on working on the Sabbath. Exodus 35:2 clearly states he should be put to death. Am I morally obligated to kill him myself?

A friend of mine feels that even though eating shellfish is an abomination (Lev. 11:10), it is a lesser abomination than homosexuality. I don't agree. Can you settle this?

Lev. 21:20 states that I may not approach the altar of God if I have a defect in my sight. I have to admit that I wear reading glasses. Does my vision have to be 20/20, or is there some wiggle room here?

I know you have studied these things extensively, so I am confident you can help. Thank you again for reminding us that God's word is eternal and unchanging.

                                                ಬಡಚ

From: Jeremy Seely <jseely@_____.com>
To: Jordan Adams <jadams@_____.net>
Sent: Thursday, June 8, 2000
Subject: Re: God's Law

Hey Jordan,

This forward is a textbook example of what's called a "straw-man" attack. Basically, it's when someone sets up a simplistic representation of the idea, work, or person they are opposed to (most often by using statements, etc. which are taken out of context or juxtaposed together to distort their meaning), one which does not represent the true nature of such idea, work, or person, and is also easily torn down and/or ridiculed—i.e. a "Straw-man." This naïve portrait is then systematically shown to be ridiculous.

Straw-men arguments usually rely exclusively on sarcasm, and are extremely effective among people who like to have their thinking done for them (as a good friend of mine says: "5% of people think, 10% think they think, and the other 85% would rather die than think").

It is clear that the person who wrote this admittedly witty straw-man argument has never actually read the entire Bible for themselves, and has never bothered to understand its message in its entirety. I've heard that same argument over and over again through the years, so this person probably heard it from someone who heard it from someone who heard it from someone, etc. Anyone who's actually read the Bible would know that this sarcastic put-down has no merit, at least in terms of true argument and debate.

"A little knowledge is a dangerous thing." So true. Straw-men attacks are incredibly destructive to truth and the search for it, because they are cop-outs and the easy way out of serious introspection and debate. Anyone with a little knowledge and a gift for wit and sarcasm can influence large numbers of people, because most people believe what they are told, and won't take the time to do some deep thinking for themselves.

On the other hand, the fundys have to share some of the blame. By making overly simplistic statements themselves about the eternal, unchanging principles of the Bible, they leave themselves open to this kind of attack. Truth is more complicated than either the fundys or their opponents make it out to be—but it IS there to be grasped.

Anyway, that's my soapbox (damn! I hate it when that happens!). As for Dr. Laura, I really can't say anything about her 'cuz I don't listen to her. Hope all is going well with you.

Take care,

Jeremy

Subject: Our Truth
Friday, June 9, 2000

Hey Jeremy,

As always, I find your letters intelligent and well formulated.

To understand how two truths for two different people can exist at the same time I find it helpful to remember the Buddhist principle of subjective and objective reality. In your subjective reality, everything (or lots) of what you read in the bible rings true for you. Everything in your soul and very fiber of your being "gets it" and feels it. You are an awesome guy, you naturally want to spread this feeling and understanding to everyone you meet. After all, for you it is the truth – right? Now check this out: there's a guy in Afghanistan reading the Koran right now - he feels it, he knows it, everything in his fiber tells him "My God! I've found you! I must spread the word!" He doesn't understand, nor may he care to understand, your interpretation of God. You feel he is misguided, misinformed or just flat wrong. If we, at this point, don't transcend our paradigm or subjective reality, we have a potential for hurting each other (in the name of God!). The dangerousness of claiming the "truth" for our culture or our religion is apparent. It can lead to arrogance, misunderstanding, and death. God does not want this. In my (subjective) reality, I'm not interested in books that claim dominion over other books. Sometimes they can be uplifting and inspiring - yes. They have some truths in them - yes but they can create dangerous tendencies in man. One of these tendencies is a searching for closure. It's natural, we want answers. If I say, "Ah hah! This is it! End of story, THIS is THE answer!" I get closure, I feel relief and now I can start making everyone see my...uh.....THE truth.

I can hear you now, "Yeah but Jordan there are absolutes!"

I do believe there are absolutes. For me, they are not found in man's interpretations. Man A's interpretations has a tendency to lead to Man B's slavery and misery. For you, the quotes from the Bible were taken out of context and paint a skewed picture. For this gentleman, Dr. Laura's use of the Bible is out of context and unfair. She feels just as strongly that she is doing the right thing. Two opposite truths existing at the same time. How?! Subjective reality. Let me highlight one more example, then I'll get off my soap box! You said "anyone who's actually read the Bible" I must ask you how much time you've spent reading the Koran, the Torah, or the Bhagad-vadgida. These books are just as holy and sacred to hundreds of millions of people as the Bible is to you. I do not say this as a put down or some kind of "one-upsmanship" I say it to illustrate the tendency we all have all the time to "paradigm" and claim the truth for all.

If you choose, meditate on this, pray on this, and get your own answers.
I know they'll be right for you.
I'm off my soap box ole boy.

It's nice to stay in touch with you. I appreciate your staying friends with me, and hope you and Monica are doing well. I hope you can do a show soon so we can hang.

Peace and Blessings

ଷଠୟ

Sent: Friday, June 9, 2000
Subject: Re: Our Truth

Jordan,

Well said! As usual, I couldn't agree more with so much of what you have to say.

"The dangerousness of claiming the "truth" for our culture or our religion is apparent. It can lead to arrogance, misunderstanding, and death."

—Not only can, but HAS led to all those things. That is one of the saddest things about humanity. Something that is meant to bring peace, serenity, enlightenment is turned around to bring slavery, death, and injustice. The only thing I would add is the question, Where does the responsibility for that lie? With the belief system, or with the people using the belief system for their own gain? Clearly I believe it to be the latter. People who crave earthly power over others will use any means to achieve it, whether it be by claiming their religion is "right" and God told them to, or by using political power, or anything else they can get their hands on. For centuries men in power have used their religion to justify acts of evilness. Unfortunately that makes people associate religion with barbarism, greed, conquest, etc. But if you look at the teachings of the religions themselves, you'll see that they all roundly denounce (with perhaps the exception of Islam and 'jihad') such acts. You can't throw out religion because of the way people have abused it. For example, Jesus said, "Follow ME." Not "Follow my people."

"Man "A"'s interpretations have always led to Man "B"'s slavery and misery."

—Here's something that I just flat out disagree with. What makes me disagree with that statement is the word 'always'. I believe this is simply not true. The people that the world regards as the most spiritual, the most religious are the ones that we recognize as those who tried to bring peace, enlightenment, a better way of life, etc. to those around them. Buddha, Krishna, Gandhi, Jesus (who, I admit, I believe was much more than these others, but for the sake of this point he belongs here), Moses, Luther, Lincoln, Confucius, Lao Tzu. These were all people who had "their truths" and yet did not use it to gain power over others. In fact, most of them are known for being a servant to others, even to the point of giving their lives. Once again, in judging any religious belief, we must not look to how those following such belief acted, but at the belief itself, how well it corresponds to reality, and if there is any objective reason to believe it.

I have spent time reading the Bhagavad Gita, the Upanishads, the Book of Mormon, the Koran, the Torah, the sayings of Buddha, the sayings of Confucius, the sayings of Bhagwan Shree Rajneesh. I must admit, not as much as I have studied the Bible, but I am familiar with them all. I found that, apart from "It just feels right to me," there is no sound <u>reason</u> to believe any of the holy books except for the Bible. I'm actually a skeptic at heart, which may sound weird coming from a believer in the Bible. But I was won over by the weight of evidence supporting the truth-claims of Jesus and the Bible. I'm really not naturally a very spiritual person, more of a meat-and-potatoes realist, but I feel compelled to believe because of the objective evidence, and that evidence has borne itself out in my life (that's what you would call the subjective reality). I find that only in Christianity do objective and subjective reality meet and intertwine. I believe that all the religions of the world have truth in them, and that all Truth comes from God, but that they reach their fullest maturity, their fullest expression, in the person and work of Jesus.

I will admit that the religion of Christianity (as well as the other major religions of the world) has been the justification for so much of the world's bloodshed and misery. That's come about from two things, in my humble opinion: first, as I mentioned earlier, the evil that comes out of men's hearts, and second, from what I would call the "religionization" of Christianity (perhaps "institutionalization" is another word that works there). You see, true Christianity, as Jesus illuminated, is not a religion at all, but a <u>relationship</u> with the Divine. It's pictured throughout the Bible in many different ways: as a marriage relationship, a parent/child relationship, a king and servant relationship, an intimate friendship, a shepherd and his sheep (not the most flattering, but it does ring true does it not?), and so on. In fact, Jesus' harshest words were reserved for the 'religious' people of His day, those that let the rituals of their belief become more important than the belief itself. True Christianity is a vibrant, living relationship with the God who created the entire Universe out of a Love so unending that we cannot even begin to fathom it, not a staid, stolid list of rules, regulations, rituals, and condemnations of outsiders. Unfortunately (or fortunately, depending on whether you're a half-empty or half-full kind of guy), you'll find both in this world today. As one of my pastors used to say: "The Bible sheds a lot of light on Christianity."

Finally, I will say that I *have* meditated and prayed about this kind of thing many, many times over the years, and it has done two things for me. It has continued to reaffirm my belief in the ultimate truth of Jesus, and at the same time it has opened my mind to people of other faiths, allowed me to see that the spark of Divine Truth can be found everywhere, and that God will not be boxed in to any formula, ritual, creed, whatever. He's way too big for that—and that's the understatement of a lifetime.

Take care and don't stay too deep for too long, you'll run out of air! =)

Jeremy

Truth poorly defended loses not its truthfulness;

likewise Falsehood aptly defended loses not its falsity.

Subject: Re: Our Truth
Monday, June 12, 2000

Hey Jeremy,

As always, I loved receiving your thoughtful response.
You have revitalized my hope for genuine discourse with a person of the Christian faith. I in no way mean that to sound like a slam. It's just that I moved here from the Bible Belt—Tampa, Florida—and have dealt with my fair share of "fundys". In fact one of my longer-term girlfriends was a "fundy". We loved each other deeply, but hit quite a few walls.

Thank you for correcting me that Man A's interpretations have always led to Man B's slavery and misery," is not necessarily always true. You're right of course. Using the word "always" is using an absolute. Okay, I can't make that statement. Let me say it's dangerous and wrong for me to impose my interpretations on you.

I am very impressed at the time you spent studying the great works of our time. Also "humbled and embarrassed" at my assumption that you hadn't. Though I haven't spent anything like the time you have, I'd like to share with you some of the Bible passages that I love:

> *"All these things you can do and greater." "The kingdom of heaven is within." "Let he who is without sin be the one to cast the first stone."*

These may be out of context, and I couldn't tell you which book they're from, but I can tell you they resonate with me.

Here's the part of Christianity I'm not in synch with:
You listed some of the great spiritual masters of our time.
Buddha, Krishna, Moses, and I'll throw in Mohammed.
You said Jesus was much more. Much more what? Do you see how much of a slander it is to a Muslim or a Jew to say his or her God isn't a "real" God, but yours is? How insulted or hurt are you if someone says Jesus isn't a God? He's a man just like Mohammed was a man, and just like Moses was a man? You see, we all become positioned. We all become passionate and convinced the other person needs convincing. That's what starts wars in my reality; this is not what God wants us to do. Fighting over the path is dumb. Just get there.

Here's something you wrote that I love:

> "religionization" of Christianity (perhaps "institutionalization" is another word that works there). You see, true Christianity, as Jesus illuminated, is not a religion at all, but a *relationship* with the Divine. It's pictured throughout the Bible in many different ways: as a marriage relationship, a parent/child relationship, a king and servant relationship, an intimate friendship, a shepherd and his sheep (not the most flattering, but it does ring true does it not?), and so on. In fact, Jesus' harshest words were reserved for the 'religious' people of His day, those that let the rituals of their belief become more important than the belief itself. True Christianity is a vibrant, living relationship with the God who created the entire Universe out of a Love so unending that we cannot even begin to fathom it, not a staid, stolid list of rules, regulations, rituals, and condemnations of outsiders. Unfortunately (or fortunately, depending on whether you're a half-empty or half-full kind of guy), you'll find both in this world today. As one of my pastors used to say: "The Bible sheds a lot of light on Christianity.

GOOD stuff! and so true. In Buddhism, even saying "so true" is arrogant and "positioned" because that's an imposition of my subjective reality on your reality so let me say in my experience I am much more about my living, current, relationship with God as well.

Let me quote you again:

> I find that only in Christianity do objective and subjective reality meet and intertwine. I believe that all the religions of the world have truth in them, and that all Truth comes from God, but that they reach their fullest maturity, their fullest expression, in the person and work of Jesus.

I love it... I am glad you found that kind of peace.

Let me give you something to chew on. I have found that objective and subjective reality seldom meet. It's sort of like a matter/anti-matter kinda thing. You see, as soon as you said: "O.K. this is it! This is the way it is!" you jumped over to subjective reality. Everything relating to your spirituality is now "subject" to that paradigm. In a way, your "vessel" is now closed to other expressions of God, in a way you're closed to other opportunities. You become the judge, basing all your decisions and opinions on your pre-judged set of, if I may quote you: "a staid, stolid list of rules, regulations, rituals, and condemnations of outsiders."

In my opinion, God is much bigger than any religion. I think his love is everywhere. God, to me, is omnipotent and omnipresent. God is inside and outside all interpretations of God including the interpretations called Christianity and Buddhism. A Buddhist wouldn't get mad at me for that statement. Would a Christian? God is all-powerful, she's in me, and he's in you. I know this may sound sacrilegious to you, but go look in the mirror, smile that awesome Jeremy smile, and say hello to God. Then forgive yourself for ever thinking God would judge you. God would have forgiven you for this, but he never judged you in the first place. His love is unconditional.

In closing, I want to say again that I experience my time and conversation with you as a blessing from God.

Love,
Jordan

ଛଓ

Sent: Thursday, June 15, 2000
Subject: This letter is as long as the Bible!

Jordan,

Thanks for the stimulating dialogue! I love talking about this stuff. By the way, I had no idea that Florida was in the "Bible Belt." I always assumed that was pretty much a Southern thing (yeah, I know Florida is technically in the south, but you know what I mean). Very interesting.

I do believe that Jesus was much more than Krishna, Buddha, etc. You asked me much more what and then went on to say that Jesus was a man like the others. That's where I mean He was much more. I believe that Jesus was God, whereas Moses, Buddha, Krishna and the others were men. I believe this because Jesus claimed it, and then proved it with his resurrection, which I believe really did happen (and which is also the most verifiable event in all of ancient history). You see, unfortunately, one can only claim that Jesus was merely a wise Teacher if he/she is ignorant of the sayings and works of Jesus. You relayed to me some passages from the Bible that you liked (all of which were spoken by Jesus, and which I like too). Here's some more things he said:

"I tell you the truth, before Abraham was born, I am!" John 8:58 ("I am" is the English translation of the Name God used of Himself—"Yahweh"—when He spoke to Moses at the burning bush—it is considered so sacred that Jews—even today—do not speak it.)

"I am the way and the truth and the life. No one comes to the Father except through me." Jn 14:6

"Anyone who has seen me has seen the Father." Jn 14:9 (Later on in the New Testament, Jesus is referred to as the "exact representation of God." This concept is clearly and unequivocally differentiated throughout the entire Bible from the New Age concept of the universal godhood of all mankind, i.e. "I Jeremy am God.")

"Do not think that I have come to abolish the Law or the Prophets; I have not come to abolish them but to fulfill them." Matthew 5:17 (And what do the Prophets have to say? Among other things: *"For to us a child is born, to us a son is given.....And he will be called Wonderful Counselor, Mighty God, Everlasting Father, Prince of Peace."* [Isaiah 9:6] How many kids do you know whose nickname was Mighty God? Before the Dead Sea Scrolls were discovered, many people claimed that prophecies such as this were obviously written in much later by followers of Jesus. The scrolls, however, date back 150 years before Christ, and all the prophecies, indeed nearly all the Old Testament, exists on them exactly as it does today.)

"All authority in heaven and on earth has been given to me." Matt. 28:18

"I am [the Messiah], and you will see the Son of Man sitting at the right hand of the Mighty One and coming on the clouds of heaven." Mark 14:62

"Come to me, all you who are weary and burdened, and I will give you rest." Matt. 11:28

"In this world, you will have trouble. But take heart! I have overcome the world." Jn 16:33

"No one has ever gone into heaven except the one who came from heaven—the Son of Man." Jn 3:13

And of course the most famous of all Jesus' sayings, John 3:16: *"For God so loved the world that he gave his one and only Son, that whoever believes in him shall not die but have eternal life. For God did not send his Son into the world to condemn the world, but to save the world through him. Whoever believes in him is not condemned, but whoever does not believe stands condemned already because he has not believed in the name of God's one and only Son. This is the verdict: Light has come into the world, but men loved darkness instead of light because their deeds were evil."*

Jesus clearly had a sense that He was much more than a specially enlightened human being. He pronounced Himself equal with God. Equal With GOD!!! Just take a moment to ruminate seriously on that. Imagine the most <u>extreme</u> arrogance in making such a statement if it were not in fact true! Imagine someone today making statements such as these. We would immediately write them off as OBVIOUSLY mentally ill—in fact we would probably say they have a Messiah or Christ complex! Now think about Jesus. Does He strike you as one who was mentally ill? Did Jesus the Christ have a Christ-complex? Or perhaps He was lying when He pronounced Himself equal with God? In which case He's not really much of a moral Teacher is He? He inspired people to die for Him on the belief that He was God in human form. If he was lying, we should stop venerating him immediately. Or maybe, just maybe, he never really said those things, or his disciples distorted his words, taking them out of context. That's where most of the disbelievers in Jesus stand today. Unfortunately for them, there is a <u>mountain</u> of evidence supporting the veracity of the Bible and the sayings of Jesus—something which if you're interested I can write more about later or point you to some reference materials. It's been said that if you throw out the Bible as being an unreliable source of historical information, you must throw out EVERY SINGLE PIECE of ancient literature that exists as being completely and utterly worthless as a record of history. Let me close out this paragraph with a quote from C.S. Lewis: *"A man who was merely a man and said the sort of things Jesus said would not be a great moral teacher. He would either be a lunatic—on a level with the man who says he is a poached egg—or else he would be the Devil of Hell. You must make your choice. Either this man was, and is, the Son of God: or else a madman or something worse. You can shut him up for a fool, you can spit at Him and kill Him as a demon; or you can fall at his feet and call Him Lord and God. But let us not come with any patronizing nonsense about His being a great human teacher. He has not left that open to us. He did not intend to."* [1]

I do understand and am sensitive to the beliefs of others even while disagreeing with them. I would never say to a Jew or a Muslim that their god isn't a real god. Instead I do what I do here, argue in favor of Jesus, rather than against Mohammed or what not. But in truth, I myself am not offended in the slightest when people tell me Jesus isn't God. If you could see some of the correspondence I've carried on with other people, I think you would see that I've heard it all—people literally calling me a nutcase in desperate need of deprogramming, and a waste of their time, all while I'm trying to carry on a civilized, rational, intelligent dialogue like the one we've been having here. Jesus never got involved in arguments with people who disputed His claims—He simply let them walk away. He knew, and so do I, that some people just don't want to be a part of what He's about, and trying to shove it down their throats just makes it worse. I know that there are billions of people who don't believe what I do, so it doesn't bother me to hear someone say that. What bothers me (and grieves me considerably) is when someone won't at least be open-minded enough to consider the evidence when given the opportunity and judge for themselves. I am quite passionate about my beliefs, and you sound as if you are too. I don't think that's a bad thing, and I don't think it always leads to war, whether literal or metaphorical. Just look at our example, and conversations like this are happening in thousands of places in every country in the world without resorting to violence or ill will. But you are right that fighting does take place and I'm right there with you that this is not what God wants. Fighting over the path is absolutely dumb. In my opinion, *debating and discussing* what the path is, or whether there is one at all, is a worthy occupation.

I like what you said about objective/subjective reality seldom meeting. Very perceptive. In one sense you are absolutely right. As soon as I said "This is it!" I did cross over the gulf from objective to subjective belief. The theological term for that is faith (*"the substance of things hoped for, the evidence of things not seen"* Hebrews 11:1 KJV). And it is true that the vessel of my spirit (I love that analogy) is in some part closed to other opportunities. I concede that to you—there are certain truth-claims that I do reject as being untrue. I don't however, see this as being a negative thing. If I may use an analogy here—when you accept the truth-claims of mathematics, namely that 2+2=4 etc., you by necessity reject the truthfulness of the claim that 2+2=5. You come to "place your faith" so to speak in the truthfulness of the mathematical system (i.e. crossing over from objective reality to subjective belief) and become closed off to other truth-claims that contradict the system. But obviously you can see that this is a positive thing, because if everyone did math the way that it "felt right for them" we would never get anywhere! Imagine NASA trying to send man to the moon when one guy says "2+2=4", another says "No! 2+2=5!" and still another says "Hey, quit fighting over it! Go with whatever works for you. You're both right! Now let's just get along and go to the moon, huh?" You can see the absurdity of the situation. In the case of mathematics, we put our subjective trust in the current system because it is based on objective truth, something that doesn't change no matter how you feel about it, and something which has proven itself to be true in our experience. When you follow the rules of math, everything makes sense. You see, faith is only as good as the object in which it is placed. For example, you can have all the faith in the universe that a quarter-inch of ice will hold your weight if you decide to go ice-skating on a pond in Ohio, but the objective reality is that it won't, and you will become very wet, maybe even very dead! On the other hand, you can have nothing but the smallest smidgen of faith that three feet of ice will hold your weight on said pond, and no matter how you feel about it, if you skate on that ice, it will hold your weight. That's the meaning of Jesus' saying that if you have faith as small as a mustard seed you will be able to say to the mountain "Throw yourself into the sea" and it will. Because faith in Jesus, no matter how small and fragile, is faith in an objective reality.

Christianity is a subjective relationship with the living God of the universe that is based upon an objective reality which doesn't change. The cornerstone of that reality is the Resurrection of Jesus, for if that happened then everything He said is shown to be true—if it didn't happen, then, as Paul says, "our faith is futile" and Christianity is literally nothing more than a sham religion. There is no middle ground here, and the more you study it the more you come to realize that. If you happen to have access to a Bible, I Corinthians chapter 15 is a superb elocution of this. Christianity is an all-or-nothing belief, as C.S. Lewis alluded to in the quote I mentioned above. That's not to say that all other belief systems are completely and utterly filled with lies and untruth—there is much wisdom to be gained from all religions—but like I said in my last letter, it does mean that ultimate Truth is found only in Jesus. I know personally how unsettling that is. It's a major stumbling block to many people who want a feel-good religion. But I'm more interested in Truth than in feeling good. As the Bible says, *"It is a terrible thing to fall into the hands of the living God"* (Heb 10:31 NLT). Terrible in the sense that it's damn scary to do, on so many levels.

By the way, I didn't mean to imply that you are interested in merely feeling good. It's pretty obvious from our letters that you are profoundly sincere in your beliefs and I think that's great—even though I disagree with them—because far too many people out there live unexamined lives when it comes to spirituality. It's like a breath of fresh air talking about these things with you, even though I don't agree with you!

You said that you are "much more about your living, current, relationship with God as well." Excellent! Me too! But here's where we part ways—it's best summed up, as usual, by Jesus: *"God is spirit, and his worshipers must worship in spirit AND IN TRUTH."* (Jn 4:24 [emphasis mine]) I think it's fantastic that you have the desire to worship God with your spirit, that puts you well ahead of the majority of people—Americans, at least (forgive the rampant generalization I just made but I do believe it to be true). But, to me, worshipping something that isn't True has little eternal, ultimate purpose.

You also believe that God's love is unconditional. Obviously, being a Christian, I agree with you with all my being. Here's a question, though. What about those who won't be loved by God? Those who refuse His passion? Will God force it on them—take away their free will and force them to exist in eternity with someone they don't want to be with? Imagine being married to someone you hate…for all eternity! Again, C.S. Lewis: *"There are only two kinds of people in the end: those who say to God, 'Thy will be done,' and those to whom God says, in the end, 'Thy will be done.'"* [2] And what about the truly evil people of our history like Hitler, Stalin? Are they never to be judged for the atrocities they perpetrated? Will God really just say to them with a twinkle in His eye, "It's okay boys—I love you." What will God say to those who were destroyed by people such as these? "Hey, don't worry about it. I love them!" That goes against the grain of everything that makes us human. Even the principle of karma, which is actually quite biblical, militates against this! I believe the answer to this question lies in the fusing of God's unquenchable love with His unquenchable justice—two things that are imbued into every human being are the need for love and the need for justice. Perhaps, being white males, we have a harder time understanding the inherent need for justice since we've never endured truly monumental injustice, although you can feel the prick of it from time to time—when you get an unwarranted parking ticket, when you're cheated out of something, whatever.

Is love without justice truly love? Can a parent who lets their child do whatever they want without reprimanding them truly be called a loving parent? Does a wife who doesn't get angry when her husband sleeps around truly love him? Does a man who doesn't want justice for his female friend who was raped truly love her?

Finally (finally!), don't worry. I'm not offended by your comment about the difficulty in holding genuine discourse with a Christian. I am saddened, but not surprised, to hear that, saddened especially that I've heard it many times over the past few years. It seems that a large portion of the Christian church in America has become "asleep in the light," has become "religious" in the negative sense that Jesus railed against. Thankfully that's not the case 100% here in this country, although certain high-profile people make it seem like that. And thankfully, it's not that way across the globe, either. I'm thinking especially of the church in China, which seems to be vibrant, alive, and growing monumentally, even in the face of communist persecution. It wasn't always the case, you know, that the word "Christian" conjured up the image of an old white man thumping his Bible and bashing everyone who wasn't just like him (a stereotype, to be sure, but I do believe that all stereotypes contain a grain of truth to them). Many of the most intelligent people of all history were Bible-believing Christians—in fact, the entire modern-day scientific method was invented by Christians, in an effort to "think God's thoughts after Him." There was also a time when "to show Christian charity" actually meant something, and was a complimentary phrase.

Anyway, good Lord I've talked quite long enough. You could have read

War & Peace instead! But I truly enjoy the opportunity to talk about the spiritual things with you. I'm sure I'll talk to you before then, but have a great 4th of July weekend. Take care, and God bless!

Jeremy

"The real question isn't whether we descended from monkeys - it's when are we going to stop?"
(I found that on some website, and thought it was funny) =)

Subject: Re: This letter is as long as the Bible!
Friday, June 23, 2000

Well, where do I start? I guess the best place is to say that no matter what I say I do not seek to invalidate your thoughts or to change your feelings. It's very clear to me that you have found the great peace and comfort that comes from a relationship with and understanding of Spirit. I must say that we do have a parting of the ways (or an agreement to disagree) on some of the fundamentals.

I give no books or words authority over my relationship with the Almighty Divine which always has and always will live in you, me, and every other living creature on this planet. When it comes down to it, I care not a lick about any of the "passed down" books and words of our times. Yes, there's beauty in them and certain truths to be found, but they will never take precedence over my personal relationship with God. No, I don't believe any book ever takes priority over my direct line to God.

I don't believe any book is the exact word of God. I don't believe any book is an infallible guide to be blindly followed and ignorantly obeyed. I will name just a few of the many reasons I feel this way. First, God loves us too much and wouldn't do this to his children; if we didn't have to think for ourselves, our minds would atrophy. I also believe as soon as a message goes from the spirit to "the hand" it is corrupted by subjectivity and all or most of the frameworks and paradigms to which the catholic churchmen (1st testament), or whomever is writing whatever message, are subject to at the time. A good illustration of the distortion that takes place when a message is passed from person to person can be found in the game of "Operator." you may remember how it is played: People sit in a circle and one person whispers a message to the person next to them. That message is then passed down the circle. By the time it reaches the end, it is not even close to the original message! This message is brutally distorted in just 10 minutes. Can you imagine 2000 years!!??

You took a few passages from the Bible:

> "I tell you the truth, before Abraham was born, I am." ("I am" is the English translation of the Name God used of Himself—"Yahweh"—when He spoke to Moses at the burning bush—it is considered so sacred that Jews—even today—do not speak it.)

You said you had studied some of the great eastern teachings. In many of the Hindu and Buddhist scriptures, it is completely understood and illustrated what Jesus was going through and how holy it was. It would fill my heart and make all of this correspondence worth it if I could convince you to trust enough in your own meditation and prayer work to let yourself see the "I Am" that you are. Ask Jesus to guide you. The gentle voice in your head asking you to trust won't be a demon. Nothing Holy could ever be a demon. Matter cannot be anti-matter!

> "I am the way and the truth and the life. No one comes to the Father except through me."

So True trust it baby! Ask! Ask! Soap-boxy and arrogant, I'm sorry!

I disagree with something you said:

> The cornerstone of that reality is the Resurrection of Jesus, for if that happened then everything He said is shown to be true—if it didn't happen, then, as Paul says, "our faith is futile" and Christianity is literally nothing more than a sham religion. There is no middle ground here...

We have subjective interference here. In the West, it seems we have a tendency to say it's this or that. It's all or nothing. Certainly, some of the time this is true. I don't feel it's true in this instance. In the eastern "Bibles" we see spirit over flesh and flesh over spirit miracles happen all the time. It happens so much there that it doesn't even have a miraculous "feel" to it anymore. In the East, they know it's just God at work. Of course Jesus did it too! We can all do it. It's called energy. Wait til you see what energetic discoveries science makes in the next 30 years. God is so much bigger than "It's only this path." God is so much bigger than what so many of us are saying: "Our book, our path is the only way God likes you." God is bigger than our Judeo-Christian impression of him. God is larger than our Muslim interpretations of him. God is grander than our Buddhist beliefs about him.

In short (too late), God's love is bigger than our lowly human projections of him. Evidence of this of course lies in the words we often use when we talk about him: judgment, anger, wrath, holy war, condemnation, hell and the like.

I'm not interested in any of these negative human projections.

To me, God's love is unconditional. God's love is not limited in any way. Not depending on or relying on any condition in any way. If a religion or particular dogma is saying I must do or be something to be or realize X, that has now jumped over in to the camp of conditional or conditional love.

I'm tired Dude, its 1:44 a.m. I love you Brother, and love that we're connected in a deep way. I hope you're happy. Keep the faith!

ಬಒಡ

Sent: Sunday, July 16, 2000
Subject: I have to apologize for the length of this!

Hey there Jordan,

Sorry this has been so long in coming, but I've been so busy lately with my life that I haven't really had the luxury of spending an hour or two (or three or four) in front of the computer to do some deep thinking. So why don't I just dive right in right now…

First off the bat, I have to point out a blatant contradiction you used in your last letter (in a friendly way of course!). You started off by saying that you didn't seek to change my feelings, but then a few paragraphs later you said: *"This correspondence [would be] worth it, if I could convince you to trust enough in your meditation…to let yourself see the "I Am" that you are."* So which is it? Are you trying to change my feelings or aren't you? =)

By the way, just so I'm upfront about it, I *am* seeking to persuade you that my belief in Jesus is True, and I *do* hope that you will come to see that for yourself. But that's between you and God—all I can do is be the messenger, an awesome responsibility that humbles me and frightens me too, because I know how imperfect I am.

The major theme of your last response was your distaste of giving any book or books primacy in your relationship with the Almighty. I'd like to talk about that in some detail, but before I do, let me briefly respond to something else you said. You make the assertion that God *"always has and always will live in you, me, and every other living creature on this planet."* I'm a bit confused as to what you actually believe. In some of your writings it sounds as if you subscribe to a pantheistic world view, as opposed to the transcendent view of God that I believe in (where God is present everywhere in all of His creation—omnipresent—but not *identified* with His creation, in contrast to the pantheistic view that says God is the tree, the rock, Jeremy, Jordan, and so on.). But other times, you describe God as being personal (i.e. "God would have forgiven you but He never judged you in the first place.") So a little clarification would help me immensely. But in any case, I have a simple question: Why do you believe what you do? What reasons can you give me to persuade me that your view is true? Do you simply believe what you do because it 'feels right' to you, were you brought up in a household that believed these things, do you draw these beliefs from the writings/sayings of others that you believe have the authority to know what they are talking about, or what? As of right now, I have no reason to be persuaded to agree with you except on the basis of personal preference, which, in my humble opinion, is one of the worst reasons to place your faith in any religious belief.

Let me now address your reservations about holy books and give you some reasons why I *do* believe the Bible to be an authentic and complete revelation from the Divine. First of all, I agree with you completely that no book takes precedence over one's actual relationship with God. I don't worship the Bible, I worship the One that the authors of the Bible talk about. I also concur with you that no book, indeed no person and no thing, should be blindly followed and ignorantly obeyed. Let me ask a side question here: is your prejudice against "book-followers" (evidenced by the words you use in context with these people) limited only to Christians, or to Hindus and Buddhists as well as all people—Eastern, Western, Northern, and Southern—who follow holy scriptures as a guide to life? But back to the issue. Followers of Jesus are never asked or required to be blind and ignorant in their beliefs—in fact we are commanded just the opposite. Jesus commands his followers to love God with all our heart, soul, and <u>mind</u>. Peter echoes this command as he writes to the believers: *"Always be prepared to give an answer to everyone who asks you to give the reason for the hope that you have. But do this with gentleness and respect"* (1 Peter 3:15). In the book of Acts, the people of Berea are commended because, after listening to Paul preach, they went home and *"examined the Scriptures every day to see if what he said was true"* (Acts 17:11). The first apostles didn't rely on sheep-herding tactics to win people over to the faith, instead they urgently pleaded with people to believe them on this basis: *"We did not follow cleverly invented stories when we told you about the power and coming of our Lord Jesus Christ, but WE WERE EYEWITNESSES of his majesty. For he received honor and glory from God the Father when the voice came to him from the Majestic Glory, saying, 'This is my Son, whom I love; with him I am well pleased.' WE OURSELVES heard this voice that came from heaven"* (2 Peter 1:16-18 [emphasis mine]) And they didn't stop there. They appealed to their audience's OWN FIRSTHAND KNOWLEDGE of the events surrounding Christ's life, death, burial, and resurrection. In effect, they said, "We saw this happen, AND SO DID YOU!" Very different from every other holy book in existence.

Let me explain to you the reasons behind my belief in the Bible as a revelation from God, through the hand of men. I've never attempted to do this comprehensively and succinctly before, only in bits and pieces, so the challenge is going to be figuring out what to edit—that's how much stuff there is. Some excellent books that go into much greater detail, and from which I draw much, include *More Than a Carpenter* and *Evidence That Demands a Verdict*, both by Josh McDowell, *The Case for Christ* by Lee Strobel, and *Who Moved the Stone* by Frank Morison.

First, and perhaps most impressive, is the content of the Bible itself. Consider this. The Bible is not one book, but a collection of 66 books, letters books of poetry, etc. that was written:

1. Over a period of 1600 years (over 60 generations),

2. by at least 40 different authors,

3. from vastly different walks of life (kings, peasants, philosophers, fishermen, poets, scholars, medical doctors),

4. in different moods (times of great national triumph and times of utter sorrow and despair),

5. on three different continents (Asia, Africa, and Europe),

6. in three different languages (Hebrew, Aramaic, and Greek),

7. about literally hundreds of controversial subjects.

In spite of all that, when the Bible is read in toto, it is astonishingly coherent and in amazing harmony! It reads as if it is one Story (which it is), God's redemption of humanity. The Bible is a unified work, where each book complements the other and all 66 agree on the most controversial of subjects—the nature of God and the nature of Man. I double-dare you to name any other piece of literature that has ever been penned in all of human history that can lay claim to that. In fact, I bet that you can't even find <u>ten</u> people from the same country in the same time period working in the same field of study that would be able to sit together in a room and reach such harmony. Is this absolute, scientific proof that the bible is divine in origin? No, but it is tremendously powerful testimony toward that end. Professor M. Montiero-Williams spent 42 years studying Easter books and said this in comparing them to the Bible: *"Pile them, if you will, on the left side of your study table; but place your own Holy Bible on the right side—all by itself, all alone—and with a wide gap between them. For...there is a gulf between it and the so-called sacred books of the East which severs the one from the other utterly, hopelessly, and forever...a veritable gulf which cannot be bridged over by any science of religious thought."* [3]

You may be thinking, "That's pretty impressive, but how do you know that someone didn't come in and rewrite the whole thing to make it fit together?" Good question. Here's how we know:

All historical documents are basically subjected to three tests to determine their reliability and credibility. The first is known as the bibliographical test. This test attempts to determine whether, not having the original documents, the copies we do have are accurate reproductions of the original. This is determined by the number of copies in existence and the interval of time between these copies and the original. For example, the history of Thucydides (460-400 B.C.) is available to us from 8 manuscript copies (MSS) dated at the earliest about 900 A.D., about 13 centuries after he wrote the original. The history of Herodotus is in approximately the same condition. Caesar's history of the Gallic Wars was composed between 58—50 B.C. and its manuscript authority rests on nine or ten copies dating 1000 years after his death. There are no classical scholars who dispute the accuracy and reliability of these texts. The second most reliable document of antiquity is Homer's Iliad, of which we have 643 copies extant (perhaps more by now). The manuscript authority of the New Testament is embarrassing in contrast. There are more than 20,000 copies in existence today, the earliest being between 250 and 300 years after the authors' deaths (except for small scraps of several books which are dated considerably earlier). Sounds like a long time but remember that none of the other works of antiquity are in doubt, even when the interval is more than a millennium!

The Old Testament does not have the abundance of manuscript authority, but in this case that actually helps confirm the accuracy of the copies we do have, because of the care the Jewish scribes took in copying it. If one mistake was made, the entire manuscript was destroyed and work was begun again (remember, these people believed they were copying the Word of God). In fact, they gave equal authority as the original to all copies made and completed (it is staggering to read how exact the process of copying the OT was—space does not permit detail here). The Dead Sea Scrolls dramatically improved their historic reliability. As I alluded to in a previous letter, there are many direct prophecies in the Old Testament that clearly refer to Jesus. For years skeptics scoffed because the earliest MSS we had of the OT were dated about 900 A.D. They laughed and said that obviously these prophecies were written in by devout followers of Jesus who wanted to believe he was the promised Messiah. Well, those voices had to cease after 1947 when the Scrolls were found, and many (including the Isaiah scroll which contains a great deal of Messianic prophecy) were dated at c.100 B.C. One hundred years before Christ! Upon reading these scrolls, they were found to be between 95 and 99 percent pure when compared to the copies from 900 A.D. Nearly every single instance of variation between the Dead Sea Scrolls and the next earliest MSS were minor differences in spelling. The accuracy of the transmission of the Hebrew text is quoted as being "little short of miraculous." Also, "…it may safely be said that no other work of antiquity has been so accurately transmitted." [4]

The "game of operator" argument (also known as the "game of telephone") is used by thousands upon thousands of people, because it sounds so convincing. And indeed it is a powerful argument…on the surface. Unfortunately (for those that hold to it) that analogy has absolutely nothing to do with the facts of how the Bible has been handed down over the centuries. It's interesting to note that there are nearly zero scholars in the world who continue to attempt to discredit the Bible on that basis. Rather, most attempt to re-interpret the Bible to suit their own prejudices, as evidenced by the Jesus Seminar, a group of pseudo-scholars that even non-Christians berate as being a mockery.

Right now all we've shown is that the Bible we have today is the same Bible that has always been. No mention has been made of the credibility of its content. The second test given to historical works is called the internal evidence test. Literary critics still follow Aristotle's advice: *"the benefit of the doubt is to be given to the document itself, not arrogated by the critic to himself."* That basically means that you don't assume fraud or error unless the author has previously given you reason. This test has a lot to do with the author's ability to tell the truth, which is linked with their nearness to the situation, both geographically and chronologically. As I mentioned earlier, the guys that wrote the books and letters that became the New Testament were eyewitnesses of the events they wrote about, or they received their information first-hand from eyewitnesses. And before you think that they made up their stories, consider this: most of the writers of the NT died a martyr's death for their beliefs. Many people in history have given up their lives for a lie, but no one has ever give up their life for what they knew to be a lie. If Jesus did not physically rise from the dead, the disciples knew it and yet died proclaiming that very thing. Consider also the presence of hostile witnesses. Not only were believers alive at the time the NT was being written and the message of Jesus' resurrection proclaimed, unbelievers were as well. The disciples could not afford to risk inaccuracy in what they preached, not to mention willful distortion, because many were the enemies of Jesus who would have pointed out their contradictions immediately.

The third test is called the external evidence test. Basically this test asks whether other historical material confirms or denies the document being studied. Once again, the Bible passes with flying colors. Writers such as Eusebius, Irenaeus, Josephus, and Ignatius all give credence to the New Testament, and there are several other ancient texts that complement the Old Testament. Archaeological evidence can also be placed in this category, and this is where the Bible really shines. It's said, only half-jokingly, that every time a hole is dug in Israel it confirms the Bible. The archaeological evidence supporting the historicity of the Bible is so massive that we look at the few problems we do have left (and there are some) as merely waiting their turn to be resolved. Here are just a couple examples. For years, bible critics laughed at the Bible's mention of a people-group known as the Hittites. "We've been digging for years," they said, "and we've never found one shred of evidence that there were any such people called the Hittites." Well, guess what. Archaeologists eventually found the Hittites. Also, when the city of Jericho was discovered and excavated, it was discovered that the walls of the city did indeed fall out, as the bible says, which is extraordinary because city walls usually fell in. Finally, Sir William Ramsey, who is regarded as one of the greatest archaeologists of all time, set out on a mission to disprove the historical details that Dr. Luke (the author of the book of Acts and the Gospel of Luke) used in his writing. Ramsey had been brought up to believe that the book of Acts was a mid-2nd century document, not the 1st century document it purported to be. He eventually reversed his belief completely, finding that, even down to the tiniest detail, Luke was absolutely historically accurate. Ramsey, a formerly "hostile witness," went so far as to say "Luke is a historian of the first rank; not merely are his statements of fact trustworthy; he is possessed of the true historic sense; he fixes his mind on the idea and plan that rules in the evolution of history, and proportions the scale of his treatment to the importance of each incident. He seizes the important and critical events and shows their true nature at greater length, while he touches lightly or omits entirely mush that was valueless for his purpose. In short, this author should be placed along with the very greatest of historians." [5]

Fine. So the Bible is the most historically accurate document of ancient times. Does that make it the Word of God? Maybe, but maybe not. So here's some more evidence. It's called prophecy. Only one who transcends time altogether, like, say, God, would be able to tell the future. Yet that's exactly what we find in the bible. There are literally hundreds of prophecies in the bible, but I'll only deal very briefly with some of those that mention Jesus. Jesus himself appealed to Messianic prophecies to validate His message:

> *"Do not think that I came to abolish the Law or the Prophets; I did not come to abolish, but to fulfill."* (Mat. 5:17)

> *"And beginning with Moses and all the Prophets, [Jesus] explained to them what was said in all the Scriptures concerning Himself."* Luke 24:27

> *"You diligently study the Scriptures because you think that by them you possess eternal life. These are the Scriptures that testify about me, yet you refuse to come to me to have life. If you believed Moses, you would believe me, for he wrote about me. But since you do not believe what he wrote, how are you going to believe what I say?"* Jn 5:39, 46-47 [You may be satisfied to read this quote—Jesus himself says that the Scriptures are not the essence of spirituality, but merely a signpost]

I mentioned in my last letter a prophecy in Isaiah. Isaiah contains probably the highest number of prophecies about the coming Messiah. The 53rd chapter of Isaiah is perhaps the most clear prophecy in the book. You should check it out. The book of Micah explicitly states that the Messiah would be born in Bethlehem (Bethlehem Ephrathah, to be specific. There were actually two Bethlehems). Like I said earlier, the discovery of the Dead Sea Scrolls nullifies the possibility that they were all written in after the fact. For me personally, the most astounding prophecy in the Bible is the last four verses of Daniel, chapter 9. These verses give the date that the Messiah will appear. Basically it says that, from the issuing of a decree to rebuild Jerusalem there will be 483 years until the Messiah (or Anointed One) appears. It goes on to state that he will then be "cut off" (killed) and that the city, as well as the temple, would once again be destroyed. We know from history that Artaxerxes issued this decree on March 14, 445 B.C. (Once again, I am trying to be brief so I'm not going into greater detail. I strongly urge you to check out the books I referenced earlier if you're interested.) 483 years works out to be 173,880 days using the Hebrew calendar of a 360-day year. The date that corresponds to that is April 6, 32 A.D., the Sunday before Passover of that year. Today we know that day as Palm Sunday, the ONLY day in all of Jesus' ministry that he allowed himself to be worshipped by the public as the Messiah. Less than one week later, he was crucified. Less than 40 years after that, in 70 A.D., the Romans destroyed Jerusalem and leveled the Temple. How do you explain that? That's not something that you can just shrug your shoulders over. And that is just one of hundreds!

A statistician named Peter Stoner took just 8 of the 60 major messianic prophecies and estimated the likelihood that a man could fulfill them by coincidence. His figure was 1 in 10 to the 17th power (1 chance in 100,000,000,000,000,000). He illustrates this by saying "Suppose we take 10 to the 17th silver dollars and lay them on the face of Texas. They will cover all of the state two feet deep. Now mark one of these silver dollars and stir the whole mass thoroughly, all over the state. Blindfold a man and tell him that he can travel as far as he wishes, but he must pick up one silver dollar and say that this is the right one. What chance would he have of getting the right one? Just the same chance that the prophets would have had of writing these eight prophecies and having them all come true in any one man, from their day to the present time, providing they wrote them in their own wisdom." [6]

Well, there you have it. That's a drop in the bucket of why I believe the Bible to be unique among all the "holy books" of the world. I cannot deny the veritable mountain of evidence that the Bible was penned by mortal man, but forged in the mind of the Divine Himself. Once again, I don't worship the Bible. God didn't design the Bible so we would worship *it* but *Him*. All that evidence is merely a hook to give you something to hang your faith on, a way to be certain that there is a Divine Being out there who loves you, loves you so much that He was willing to die in your place so that you could be with Him forever if you so choose. And it is a choice. God's love is unconditional, exactly as you said. God loves you no matter what you do, who you are, or what you believe. God even loved Adolph Hitler. In fact, He loved Hitler more than you love your family—more than I love Monica. But love is a two-way street. Both parties must consent to be in a relationship. And both must love in *truth* as well as in spirit. If I said I loved Monica, but my image of her was a 6-foot tall, black-haired woman who wanted to be a stockbroker, you would say there's something wrong, wouldn't you? That wouldn't be real, True love, only something in my head.

Anyway, the entirety of the reason that I laid out this defense of the Bible was in hopes that you would at least open your mink to the possibility that what the Bible says about Jesus is true. After all, he is the centerpiece of the faith, not the Bible. Jesus incontrovertibly claimed to be God. There is no getting around that. He did not claim that we too were God. Anyone who says otherwise is simply (perhaps willfully) ignorant. He was killed for proclaiming that, because that was the absolute height of Jewish blasphemy, if in fact His claims were not true. But then, according to the writers of the New Testament, many of whom were personal disciples of Jesus, He rose from the grave to prove that He was all that He said He was. And, incredible as it may sound to modern ears, there is no doubt that His tomb was empty that first Easter morning. If his body were there, all it would take to crush this burgeoning movement for all time would be to haul out the corpse (Bring out'cher dead!) and parade it around the city for all to see. So, to get around that, some people said that the disciples stole the body. But that's just absolutely ridiculous! Notwithstanding the security guards that were present to prevent just such an occurrence, why on earth would they do such a thing? They could just as easily said that Jesus rose in spirit, then they wouldn't have to trouble themselves with a missing body. Not only that, but like I said earlier, all of them underwent horrible persecution because, to a man, they would not deny the bodily resurrection of Jesus. They profited absolutely nothing, from a worldly point of view, by doing this. Not only that, but how could it be possible that a group of ordinary men and women would go on to transmit the highest ethical teaching the world has ever known while at the same time conspiring with each other in a colossal lie?

Some posited that Jesus didn't actually die on the cross, merely "swooned," then came to in the coolness of the tomb. This was never really taken seriously by anyone (as far as I know), but it does provide a little humor to the debate. Imagine that Jesus, by some miracle, survived one of the most cruel forms of capital punishment ever devised. He wakes up in utter darkness, covered head to toe in bandages that were pasted over with about 50 pounds of spices which harden to form a shell around the body. Somehow, he's able to get himself into a standing position, hop over to this 2-ton stone which locks the tomb shut. Even though suffering grievous wounds, he knocks the stone over and slips past the detachment of guards standing watch. He makes his way over to where the disciples are hiding, and is somehow able to convince these guys that he is the Lord of Life, the Mighty God, and the promised Messiah! …You can obviously see why this theory died a quick death.

Let's see, what other explanations have been offered? Ah yes, the hallucination theory. This one says that everyone hallucinate seeing Jesus alive again. First of all, this brings us back to the empty tomb. Show Jesus' body, end of story. That was never done. Second of all, Jesus appeared to several people at once, and one time to a group of 500! It is a simple fact (as well as plain common sense) that people, especially in those numbers, do not hallucinate the exact same phenomenon. Today, people are saying that there was no body because Jesus was actually thrown into a mass grave, where the dogs would come and devour the corpses. But this theory completely ignores the biblical account of His burial in a special tomb, and the biblical account has proven to be reliable. Besides, if that was the case, do we really believe that this fact would not surface until two millennia later? Theories come and go, but as I said, there really is no plausible explanation except that, "on the third day, He rose again."

In your last letter, you talked about eastern scriptures referring to miracles and whatnot. Indeed, don't stop there! There are several instances in other holy books of gods dying and coming back to life. Jesus is just one of many! Right? Actually, no. All the other instances are clearly intended as myth, as fantastical stories; the Resurrection of Jesus appeals firmly, soberly, and completely to history, as an actual fact that did take place in time and space. I look at these other instances as examples of the fact that we mortals "see as through a glass, darkly." We can intuit, in some fractured and partial way, the truth about what God is like. These other stories are images and foreshadowings of the truth, a kind of worldwide sense-memory, which ultimately is consummated in Jesus. That is why all of the wisdom in all of the religions of the world is also found in Christianity, but Christianity unifies all of it and then goes much further, with God's revelation to us. Man can only go so far in intuiting the Infinite—we require the Infinite to come down to our level in order to more fully understand. And that is exactly what the Incarnation of Jesus is—the Infinite putting on the Finite to show us what He is like and how much He loves us.

I understand that you have a problem with one group of people telling another how to express themselves spiritually—imposing their beliefs and form of worship on another. I sympathize with that sentiment. I sympathize with that sentiment when the words "impose," "force," "coerce," etc. are used in that statement. But once again you are making a worldwide generalization based on a negative stereotype. You'll find millions upon millions of Christians today who are Christians by choice, and are blessed because of it. I am one of them. Yes, followers of Jesus do believe in spreading the message to all peoples of all nations and tribes, but only because it is True and He commanded us to. Just think for a moment: What if it's true? What if all the Bible says about Jesus really happened? What if He *is* very God of very God, and really *did* rise from the dead to confirm His message? Ludicrous as it sounds, that's the direction that the overwhelming abundance of facts point! If Jesus is God, and He says "I want you to tell the whole world about me," who am I to refuse?!? Like you said, God is bigger than any religion, and Jesus didn't come to found a religion. He came to show us what God is like. Jesus didn't say "Go tell the whole world that you must play pipe organ music, sing two hymns in English, kneel and sit, kneel and sit, and listen to a man wearing a certain kind of robe." No! He simply said "Tell everyone about me and about what I said and did. Then disciple them to be followers of me." It is true that the Christian church has forced "religion" on people at times throughout history, but once again, that's not Jesus' mission, only imperfect man's. Christianity is *not* rituals, rites, pipe organs, and whatnot, but a relationship with the True, Living God of the Universe as Jesus revealed to us. One does not have to give up his/her culture to follow Jesus, one does not have to become "Westernized" to follow Jesus. That is one of the biggest stereotypes people in this country hold to today. Christianity is not a Western religion—it's just the way the course of history went that it took hold in Europe, became "religionized" (of course, I'm not speaking universally of all Christians when I say that), and then was spread West as the Europeans conquered. But there are actually more Christians in China today than there are in the U.S.—and they have their own, Chinese way of worshipping Jesus. Yes, they use the Bible that we use and believe the same things we do, but they don't worship in a "Western" way. Same thing with Native American Christians, Vietnamese Christians, Nigerian Christians. Believing in Jesus doesn't suppress or take away one's cultural background, if anything it enlivens it and brings new fulfillment and consummation to it, because suddenly all your cultural ways of expressing yourself are being used to worship in spirit as well as in Truth! And what is more beautiful than that?

I truly apologize for making this so incredibly long. Take comfort in the fact that it took me MUCH longer to write than it did for you to read. =) But, like I said earlier, the challenge for me was actually not, "How much can I cram in?" but "What can I leave out?" Indeed, when I look back over this, I worry that I didn't include enough to be convincing. But, hopefully, we'll have more exchanges where we can both share more with each other.

I don't expect you to completely buy all of this as soon as you read it. Study this in greater detail. Wrestle with it. Struggle with it. Doubt it—as I have done, and continue to do. Email me some more! Meditate and pray about it in your own Jordan way, and I have confidence that if you open your mind, God's light will flood into your being more than it already has. The message of Jesus is not religion, but **FREEDOM**!

I will attest to that. Jesus has brought me life (abundant life), literal miracles, fulfillment, a sure knowledge that my life here counts, has a purpose, and will continue. Of course, I am not perfect (I am what the Bible terms a "sinner") so I don't always live that way, in perfect peace and whatnot, but in my innermost being, when all the crap gets cleared away, I know all this. And don't say, "Well that's great for you, but it's not true for me." Either it's true or it's not. If it's not true, then all my beliefs and hopes that my light and momentary troubles will work out in the end are based on a lie. But God, in His infinite wisdom and love, has provided the means for us to rationally believe in the Truth of Jesus, if we are willing. And for that, I am eternally grateful.

Blessings,

Jeremy
Truth poorly defended loses not its truthfulness;
Likewise Falsehood aptly defended loses not its falsity.

Sent: Wednesday, July 19, 2000
Subject: Re: I have to apologize for the length of this!

Beautiful Jeremy, just beautiful. I have a new respect for you and your beliefs.

It will take me awhile to get back to you due to my hectic schedule, but know that I will study your letter and enjoy it immensely.

You are a great guy. Thanks for your caring and passion.

Peace and Blessings Brother.

ಬಬ

From: Jeremy Seely <jeremy_seely@_____.com>
To: Jordan Adams <jadams@_____.net>
Sent: Saturday, July 22, 2000
Subject: Re: Fw: Who was Jesus? A little humor!

Scholars have long debated the exact ethnicity and nationality of Jesus. Recently, at a theological meeting in Rome, scholars had a heated debate on this subject. One by one, they offered their evidence…

THREE PROOFS THAT JESUS WAS MEXICAN
1.   His first name was Jesus
2.   He was bilingual
3.   He was always being harassed by the authorities

But then there were equally good arguments that…..

JESUS WAS BLACK
1.   He called everybody "brother"
2.   He liked Gospel
3.   He couldn't get a fair trial

But then there were equally good arguments that…..

JESUS WAS JEWISH
1.   He went into His Father's business
2.   He lived at home until he was 30
3.   He was sure his mother was a virgin, and his mother was sure he was God

But then there were equally good arguments that…..

JESUS WAS ITALIAN
1. He talked with his hands
2. He had wine with every meal
3. He used olive oil

But then there were equally good arguments that.....

JESUS WAS A CALIFORNIAN
1. He never cut his hair
2. He walked around barefoot
3. He started a new religion

But then there were equally good arguments that.....

JESUS WAS IRISH

1. He never got married
2. He was always telling stories
3. He loved green pastures

But perhaps the most compelling evidence was that.....

JESUS WAS A WOMAN
1. He had to feed a crowd at a moment's notice when there was no food.
2. He kept trying to get the message across to a bunch of men who JUST DIDN'T GET IT
3. Even when he was dead, he had to get up because there was more work for him to do.

Subject: Re: Fw: Who was Jesus?
Sunday July 23, 2000

Hey there, Brother. Well that last letter you sent along certainly was not "flimsy" in either volume or substance!

You are right of course in your perceptive awareness of my contradiction:

> *First off the bat, I have to point out a blatant contradiction you used in your last letter (in a friendly way of course!). You started off by saying that you didn't seek to change my feelings, but then a few paragraphs later you said: "this correspondence (would be) worth it, if I could convince you to trust enough in your meditation...to let yourself see the 'I*

Am' that you are." So which is it? Are you trying to change my feelings or aren't you? =)

I like to think I am objective, but I am not. The truth is I never can be. The very fact that I am in the flesh means I'll always be subject to my "local reality."

Thanks (I think) for bringing this sometimes-painful lesson back to the forefront of my consciousness. I will come back to this theme in just a minute, but would like to try to clarify my feelings on this first:

In some of your writings it sounds as if you subscribe to a pantheistic world view, as opposed to the transcendent view of God that I believe in (where God is present everywhere in all of His creation—omnipresent—but not identified with His creation, in contrast to the pantheistic view that says God is the tree, the rock, Jeremy, Jordan, and so on.). But other times, you describe God as being personal (i.e., "God would have forgiven you but He never judged you in the first place."). So a little clarification would help me immensely.

My personifying God is for the sake of dialogue. Also, as you may have guessed with me being a progressive, I would never use the term "he" when addressing God if it weren't the standard and pre-agreed to term. This again for the pragmatism of speaking the same language. You addressed the view to which I subscribe. I do my best (most of the time unsuccessfully) not to subscribe to any "view". In my experience, as soon as I subscribe, I nullify a lot of other people's subscriptions, or conversations, with God. I want to keep trying hard not to do that… I would never presume to guess the millions of ways God reveals every day. So to your question, am I pantheistic or transcendent? **YES...**

If I'm reading you correctly, you're saying God is everywhere but not all the way everywhere. In other words, if God were the ocean, and you then scooped out a bucket of ocean water, and made it local, the ingredients now have somehow changed?

Why do you believe what you do? What reasons can you give me to persuade me that your view is true? Do you simply believe what you do because it 'feels right' to you, were you brought up in a household that believed these things, do you draw these beliefs from the writings/ sayings of others that you believe have the authority to know what they are talking about, or what? As of right now, I have no reason to be persuaded to agree with you except on the basis of personal preference, which, in my humble opinion, is one of the worst reasons to place your faith in any religious belief.

Sadly, this statement of yours points out just what a failure I've been at not judging your way of speaking and listening to God.
I have blown it. I apologize. You obviously have felt my desire to have you see and understand my connection - in other words to see things my way. :)
I guess, and this goes back to my first point, it's just plain impossible not to insert our own stuff when interpreting or trying to communicate about God. This, in my opinion, is the very reason we always thrust our take on God on to a different people. It's terrifying to think we may not have all the answers. It's terrifying to think the whole thing may just be a great big huge projection. Think about it for a minute Jeremy. What if, just what if, while the Native Americans were praying to God *Their* way, and we came in and did what we did to them in the name of *conversion*, God got mad. After all, they were in the middle of talking to him and we came in and interrupted them and then slaughtered them. Slaughtered them! A holocaust! To get them to talk to God **our** way. In my opinion, God was crying when that happened. I know right now you're saying: *"I agree that was wrong and I agree with you that God was crying too."* Well that's great that you feel that way Jeremy, but sooner or later, you're going to have to reconcile that it's the *I know I'm right and in the end you're wrong philosophy* that gives us the false belief that we're justified in conversion. That we somehow have Divine permission to do these things. It's this egocentric, paternal, subjective, localized myth that creates these holocausts in the first place.

In my opinion, **No** *Culture Has a Monopoly on Truth, or God*. That goes for any ethic, be it Muslim, New Thought, Christianity, Judaism, Buddhism, Zen, Hinduism, whatever.....

I must stop now; I wish I had time for more.

Let me close by answering one more question. You asked if I believed what I do based on my feelings.

Yes.

Yes, I do Jeremy, based on my feelings of love for God.

Blessings! My Dear Pen Pal!

☙❧

Sent: Monday, September 25, 2000
Subject: As I was saying…=)

Hola! How's life over in Jordan land? Hope all is well.
Well, I'm picking up this spiritual discussion again after a long pause—forgive me—so I'm hoping that you remember what we were talking about. Hopefully you've saved our emails so you can return to them if need be. In case you haven't but would like to peruse them again, I have copies of all of them I can send to you. I keep just about everything that I send and receive that has any substance or sentimental value.

Many times you have berated yourself for failing to take a completely neutral stance in this discussion by attempting to persuade me to see it your way. I understand that you hold that to be a cardinal sin in your life, but please don't feel bad on my account. That doesn't bother me one iota. Why do we talk about these things if not to pursue truth? If not to sharpen each other's thinking and perhaps aid the enlightenment of each other? I don't feel shame in the slightest degree when attempting to persuade you that Jesus is THE way to God in these times. Because I believe it to be true. And I don't think you should feel shamed when attempting to convince me of what YOU believe to be true. After all, if you really do believe it's true, shouldn't people know it? So please don't feel bad for trying to "show me the error of my ways." ;)

In fact here's what you said:

> *I guess, and this goes back to my first point, it's just plain impossible not to insert our own stuff when interpreting or trying to communicate about God.*

I think you're right. I think it is impossible not to add our own prejudices, desires, etc. to our view of God. But I don't think that this makes it impossible to know ANYTHING about the truth of God.

Also, thanks for giving me clarification about your view of God. I had a feeling that you were, in fact, a pantheist and merely using personal God-language to facilitate our communication, and I appreciate the gesture. But you say that you try to refrain from subscribing to any particular view. While a noble gesture of compassion and open-mindedness to people with differences of opinion, I hope you realize that this is a logical and practical impossibility. The view that you have no view is itself a view. Understand? Your attempt not to subscribe to any view belies the fact that underneath that statement is <u>the view</u> that it is more important to be "tolerant" than to be certain. Or else <u>the view</u> that there are many views. A corollary is this: Many people say that there is no absolute truth. That's an absolute statement! They're saying "It is absolutely true that there is no absolute truth."

> *If I'm reading you correctly, you're saying God is everywhere but not all the way*

everywhere. In other words, if God were the ocean, and you then scooped out a bucket of ocean water, and made it local, the ingredients now have somehow changed?

This is exactly what I am NOT saying. God is NOT the ocean. God made the ocean. His spirit is present everywhere IN the ocean, but He is not THE OCEAN. In some ways God is like the great Computer Programmer in the sky. He created this infinitely and wonderfully complex computer program: the universe. He has absolute dominion over it, since He wrote the code. In fact He can break in and change the code whenever He wants to - miracles. That's called omnipotence. And since He is infinite, His spirit is in some mystical, mysterious sense present everywhere at once in this finite universe. Obviously that's omnipresence. Since He is infinite, He can know absolutely everything that there is to know from our perspective - omniscience. Omniscience includes knowing the future as well. To God, the future is not the future, since He is outside of Time altogether. Words like today, yesterday, and tomorrow have no meaning whatsoever when applied to God (and by the way, that's why prophecies in the Bible are an integral part in making the case that the Bible originated from God, originated from outside our time domain. Only someone outside of Time altogether would be able to foretell the future).

Argh. I get so frustrated when trying to explain these concepts. They are so high above our ability to grasp that they can only be apprehended, not comprehended. C.S. Lewis was gifted with the incredible ability to make weighty, infinite concepts like these understandable to anyone - I would highly recommend reading his book *Mere Christianity*. But one of the main problems I see that we as people have in coming to terms with the qualities of God is that we look below ourselves in order to construct our view of God, we look no higher than our own understanding in order to build our box for God to fit into (pretty ridiculous). We should look above ourselves, to higher levels of complexity and reality that we are not fully knowledgeable of in order to attempt to come to terms with God's qualities. How can the finite completely understand the infinite?

Lewis is fantastic in illustrating this. He says, in summary, that a two-dimensional being (length and width) would be able to apprehend the existence of a third dimension (height) and have some knowledge of it, but could never fully comprehend existence in three dimensions. In the same way we are like that 2-D person. We can know some things about God, especially if He comes down to our level and teaches us about Him, but we can never fully understand the depth of His infiniteness.

I don't know why I spent so much time elaborating on that. I have a feeling that you already agree with me on this.

I really, truly do understand your desire not to presume the many ways in which God communicates with people, and your stern objection to people saying "This is the way." That is an issue that, honestly, I struggle with every single day of my Christian life. I can't tell you how many times I have laid awake at night wondering and wrestling with this. In the end I can only rest on one thing. Jesus said it, and I believe Him—for all the reasons I elaborated on in that tome that was my last response. In the end, He proved what He said by rising from the dead, just as He said He would. And I also rest in the fact that the Bible declares God to be absolutely and perfectly just, and absolutely and perfectly loving. So I trust that whatever happens to us when we die, everyone will look back and say "That was the right thing." I can't "prove" that, and sometimes I don't even feel that; it takes faith—believing in that which is invisible (not that which is illusory! There's a big difference!!) But I believe that God is eminently trustworthy. That's the best answer I can give. I hope it is enough, because we're not likely to get a better one.

> *What if, just what if, while the Native Americans were praying to God Their way, and we came in and did what we did to them in the name of conversion, God got really mad. After all, they were in the middle of talking to him, and we came in and slaughtered them, slaughtered them! A holocaust! to get them to talk to God our way. In my opinion God was crying that day. I know right now you're saying: "I agree that was wrong and in my opinion I agree with you that God was crying too." Well that's great that you feel that way Jeremy, but sooner or later, you're going to have to reconcile that it's the I know I'm right and in the end you're wrong philosophy that gives us the false belief that we're justified in conversion. That we somehow have Divine permission to do these things. It's this ego-centric, paternal, subjective, localized myth that creates these holocausts in the first place.*

No no no! <u>Nowhere</u> does the belief that I'm right and you're (at least partially) wrong give me Divine permission to subdue you. The one does not lead inexorably to the other, and in fact have no connection whatsoever. It is truly a "false belief" as you astutely stated. The fact that some people have used that as a pretext in order to satisfy their thirst for power does not in any way validate that point. There is no "reconciliation" between the "I'm right" philosophy and the justification of slaughter whatsoever, unless your philosophy already includes the justification of slaughter. Unless that's the case, it's comparing apples and oranges.

This actually leads me right into my next point. If nothing else comes from this correspondence, I hope you understand this part. You say that your beliefs about "God" come from your feelings of love for "God". Think for a moment on the very serious ramifications of basing your God-beliefs on your feelings, and giving credence to everyone else's feelings about "God" without making judgments. Where do you get the right to judge what happened to the Native Americans, or the Africans, or whoever, as being wrong? Just imagine hypothetically that the European conquerors actually DID believe wholeheartedly in converting people to Christ by the sword if necessary (I don't believe for a minute that the rape of the Native Americans had very much at all to do with spiritual belief—I believe it had to do with power, dominion, and money, sometimes using religion as a pretext. Anyone with even a passing knowledge of the Bible would know what an utterly UN-biblical thing that is). What if I told you that I FEEL that God is telling me that I'm supposed to burn witches? Or if I FEEL that God is telling me to kill you? Or I FEEL that God wants homosexuals to burn in hell? Or if I FEEL that God approves of me blowing up an embassy? Who are you to tell me I'm wrong? That I'm Narrow-minded? That I'm a fundy? Do you see? When you base your entire view of God on your feelings, there is no end to what you can justify! AND THAT IS EXACTLY WHAT WE HAVE SEEN HAPPEN! Plus, when you say that you endeavor to let everyone believe how they want, you have absolutely no right whatsoever to condemn ANYTHING as wrong!

In the end, feelings cannot, indeed <u>must</u> not, be the sole determiner of our relationship to God. After all, on a milder scale than that last paragraph, what if my feelings change tomorrow? Does that mean that God has suddenly changed with me? Don't you see how ludicrous it is to say that you believe in God based on what your feelings tell you? Don't get me wrong. I'm not saying feelings are useless. They are a vital part of what makes us human. But feelings are like water. Essential for life, but pretty much useless unless held in some kind of container.

Anyway, I am highly curious as to what you thought of my last letter to you. You really didn't comment on its contents except to acknowledge the thoughtfulness which went into it composition. Have I convinced you of anything? Do you disregard all of it? Are you still pondering it? I'd really like to know. Once again, let me 'splain…no there is no time to 'splain. Let me sum up. (a little Princess Bride reference there, heh heh)

- The incredible unity and harmony of the Bible in spite of its diverse origins.
- The reliability of the manuscripts that we have today, and the

surety that the Bible we read today is the Bible that was read ages ago.

- The eyewitness accounts of Jesus' life, death, and resurrection ("we did not follow cleverly invented stories, BUT WERE EYEWITNESSES of his majesty"), and the presence of hostile witnesses.
- The testimony of archaeology.
- Prophecy in the Bible, and its uncanny accuracy.
- The failure to produce any viable alternative theories to the resurrection of Jesus, and finally,
- My own personal attestation to the difference it's made in my life.

What do you make of all that?

Have a good one—I'll see you soon, Heimschleimer!

Blessings,

Flimsea (that's Flim-ZAY)

Subject: Deep Thoughts...with Jack Handy
Tuesday October 24, 2000

Hey Jeremy,

How's life treating ya up in LALA land? You are not going to believe this, but I had a many-page many-hour treatise worked up for you, and when I saved it, it crashed. The system said, "You have performed an illegal operation," and just quit. I lost the whole thing! I guess it was God's way of telling me it was not the right letter to send :) I still cursed a bit though.

I'll start over! How's that for evidence that I really do care about and love you Dude!

Initially I was just going to send a letter that said, "I love you"....that's it.... nothing more....and let you digest it to see if you would understand it as an answer to your letter.... Do you know what I mean? Really? If not, ask me to elaborate.
Well, you'll be glad to hear I decided not to go with the short version. I think I know you fairly well at this point and I think you would rather have the "meat", no light fare for my scholarly friend, no esoteric fluff, no sir :)

So I'll get right to it: You said:

> *The view that you have no view is itself a view. Understand? Your attempt not to subscribe to any view belies the fact that underneath that statement is *the view* that it is more important to be "tolerant" than to be certain. Or else *the view* that there are many views. A corollary is this: Many people say that there is no absolute truth. That's an absolute statement! They're saying "It is absolutely true that there is no absolute truth."*

Very Nice!! Let me say I'm certain it's imperative to be tolerant, and "certainty" has certainly led to intolerance.

In response to my saying:

> *"If I'm reading you correctly, you're saying God is everywhere but not all the way everywhere. In other words, if God were the ocean, and you then scooped out a bucket of ocean water, and made it local, the ingredients now have somehow changed?"* you said:

> *This is exactly what I am NOT saying. God is NOT the ocean. God made the ocean. His spirit is present everywhere IN the ocean, but He is not THE OCEAN. In some ways God is like the great Computer Programmer in the sky. He created this infinitely and wonderfully complex computer program: the universe. He has absolute dominion over it, since He wrote the code. In fact He can break in and change the code whenever He wants to—miracles. That's called omnipotence. And since He is infinite, His spirit is in some mystical, mysterious sense present everywhere at once in this finite universe. Obviously that's omnipresence.*

We do have a disagreement here, and in this instance, you didn't read me correctly. I'm not saying God is everywhere, but not all the way everywhere. I'm saying God is *everywhere* period.

It does sound like you may agree with me though, in saying his spirit is present everywhere?

You said:

> *But one of the main problems I see that we as people have in coming to terms with the qualities of God is that we look below ourselves in order to construct our view of God, we look no higher than our own understanding in order to build our box for God to fit into (pretty ridiculous). We should look above ourselves, to higher levels of complexity and reality that we are not fully knowledgeable of in order to attempt*

to come to terms with God's qualities.

I agree Sir!

Just imagine hypothetically that the European conquerors actually DID believe wholeheartedly in converting people to Christ by the sword if necessary (I don't believe for a minute that the rape of the Native Americans had very much at all to do with spiritual belief—I believe it had to do with power, dominion, and money, sometimes using religion as a pretext. Anyone with even a passing knowledge of the Bible would know what an utterly UN-biblical thing that is).

Yes, you're right, it did have to do with all the things you listed **and** the belief that the heathens had to be converted to their way or die. I know you don't want to believe it had to do with a religious belief, especially one to which you may subscribe (who would?), but I've never seen you reconcile the fact that the "I know I'm right and in the end you're wrong" mentality almost always gives a person a belief of divine superiority and divine consent.

Let's switch tracks:

I think the Fundys and the Evangelicals miss the mark. Not only do they miss the mark, but also they can, at times, hurt true spiritual revelation.

Let me try to illustrate:

They go out of their way to say God's love is so big and awesome we couldn't possibly comprehend it. In the same breath, they tell us to think of God as a parent, and a harsh, cruel, demanding angry parent at that. A Father who will tolerate absolutely no failures in certain areas. Well what is it Fundys? A love so big I can't comprehend it, or a judgmental God? I can easily grasp the "love" they're trying to assign to God. It's easily within my comprehension zone, it even looks small to me. You know why? Cuz they're projecting their smallness on him. That's what most religions, yes even Christianity, maybe especially Christianity, have done for many a millennia. They're trying to say that not only does God *demand* worship, but also he demands it in a certain way. It's not enough that a person goes to God with a yearning, passionate, innocent, loving heart, but it must be by a particular path. If not, God will reject your love, ignore your entreaties, and indeed, condemn you to hell.

Ouch!! If you're a loving Muslim, a loving Jew, a loving Native American, it doesn't matter. God will punish you by putting you into burning fires forever!! Which way is it Evangelicals? A love so big I couldn't possibly grasp it? Or the fire and pain thing? You cannot have it both ways, cuz I'll tell ya the latter is a love easily graspable—again, not much love indeed. I'm not asking you to blindly accept that this is ludicrous. Pray about it. Ask in your prayers if God wants you to have a fearship or worship with him. Ask if god cares what way and by what path you bring your friendship and your heart to him. God doesn't care about language and path. That is a big mistake we have believed in for many many years. It hurts us, and it hurts God. Jeremy your friendship and relationship with God is a living, breathing, dynamic, growing thing. Just as our (humans) understanding of our relationship with God is the same. *It's a growing dynamic.* We're coming to a new and better understanding of the sheer magnitude of God's caring for us. The anger thing.....The judgment thing.....The fire and burning thing.......It's done. God's letting us see more now. She's letting us see that that was all ours. That was *our* notion, not hers! He never had anything to do with that. The funny part is he doesn't care that we projected all that silliness on him because a true friend (a best friend) will accept anything given in love, and forgive everything, period.

We've come to the heart of our discussions. I am not asking you to do anything; God knows I'm not in any position to do that.

I can only tell you that when I broke free from the judgment and punishment thing, I truly saw God. I wept......

I know to ask these questions of God might seem sacrilege. It is scary cuz it goes against almost every religion. It takes courage to reject every notion, every idea, every teaching of the world that says: "God would hurt you."

I'm standing here just to say it. I'm trembling now as something wells up inside me. Jeremy if you hear what I'm saying, great! I hope you're saying "maybe he's on to something?" but I know I just have to let it go. You may think me a fool, but it took a lot of courage for me to reject religion. The world had been filling my head with the scary image for so long I had a lot of anger for God. But when I got past the human fear projections, I realized it's not at all a parent, authoritarian thing. Not at all. It's a friendship. A partnership. A 24/7 working, give and take partnership. *The fear thing works well for keeping the pews warm, but not for getting closer to your best friend.*

Let me hit a couple of other points briefly cuz I'm getting tired.

In my view, Evolution and Spirituality are NOT mutually exclusive! Evolution works quite well within spiritual parameters. In fact to me, the sheer brilliance of evolution only proves God's existence.

If the fundys would stop trying to scientifically prove fairy tales, things would be a little easier on 'em. In other words: Science simply is. Science doesn't start with a notion/theory and subsequently try to force-fit everything into that parameter conveniently leaving out or ignoring the results that don't quite jibe with the original hypothesis. Good science simply looks at what is and subsequently develops the theory based on what already is.

I'm exhausted, gotta quit for now. Luv ya Buddy

ಸಂಡ

Sent: Tuesday, November 7, 2000
Subject: Deep (and long) Thoughts

Jordan,

Hey there. Here's the letter. The finished version this time, not the accidentally sent incomplete draft! ;) How do you like the new theatre space? I like the look of the room itself, but I kinda miss the Mezz. Okay, enough small talk—this is a long one so I'll get right to it.

In my last letter I asked you a couple questions such as what did you think of all the stuff I talked about previously ('cuz there was a whole lot of it and I didn't hear a peep of response) that you didn't answer in your last letter. I'm hoping that you had responded in your original letter, and then just forgot to put it back in, or decided not to, in your second draft after your computer crashed (definitely a tragedy of the highest order—I feel your pain! A little helpful advice that you may not need—save drafts often!). I'm still interested in hearing from you. Let me get on to responding to some of your points now.

First off, let me reiterate again (is that redundant? to 'reiterate again'? =)) that I really enjoyed reading your last letter. I feel like I was peering into deep layers of your heart regarding your feelings of spirituality. So let me try my best to respond with sensitivity to many of the points you brought up.

> *"Let me say I'm absolutely certain it's imperative to be tolerant, and "certainty" has certainly led to intolerance."*

Did you put this irony in there on purpose? I'm thinking that you did. You're right—certainty has let to intolerance, as we've discussed in previous letters—even the certainty that it's imperative to be tolerant. A lot of people who say they believe in tolerance are really hypocrites in disguise. They say they are open-minded and tolerant, but in reality they are only tolerant of those who agree with them, and open-minded only to religious views that they like. This is a HUGE pet peeve of mine—people that claim to be so "tolerant," so "progressive," so "open-minded to all," and then go on to bash Christians as being narrow-minded exclusivists, and so on. If they really were tolerant, then they would be tolerant toward people who don't believe that all religions are equal. How can people be so blind to their own lives?!?

Let me state that tolerance is incredibly important, and in reality is more a Christian virtue than anything else. As I said before in a different way, Jesus was the epitome of tolerance. He let people go their own way and believe against Him if they so desired. He didn't say that everything would was okay if you did, but He did (and does) let people walk away. Yes, tolerance, in its true meaning, is a Christian virtue. Our culture seems to have distorted and muddied the meaning of the word these days, though, as it has done with countless other words. True tolerance, as a matter of fact, is present in the very bedrock of this country—freedom of belief. True tolerance is letting others be free to believe what they choose to believe, and not persecuting them for it (obviously there are reasonable and self-evident limits to this—i.e., Jeffrey Dahmer is not free to believe in killing kids and eating them—well, actually I take that back. He's free to believe in it, but he's not free to act on it). Bu tolerance does <u>not</u> mean agreeing with everything and saying that all statements are equally valid and true. As an example, I am of the opinion that this correspondence we've been carrying out has been a great example of tolerance at work. I couldn't disagree more with some of the things you've said, and vice-versa, and I'm even trying (God willing) to persuade you to change your mind about many critical beliefs, as are you with me, but I don't think anyone could read these letters and accuse us of being intolerant toward each other. I just wanted to define terms so you knew what I meant when I talked about tolerance, and I hope you mean the same thing.

Okay, let me move on to some of the deeper, more complex issues you raised. Thanks for calling me on my statement about the European conquerors. I think you're right, and I should revise my statement a bit about their motives of conquest. I think I was just reacting to a seemingly prevalent stereotype that religion was the <u>sole</u> reason they went out to conquer, and that is what I don't believe. I think my main point still stands, though, and that is that there is no logical justification whatsoever in oppressing you because 'I'm right'. My point here is that it seems to me that you're equating all religious certainty with oppression, and I'm just saying that even though it has happened with Christianity in the past and with other religions in the present, you can't use that as an argument against religious certainty in itself, because the two are not logically related.

The other point is that, whatever the reasons for all the evils that have been done in the name of Christ over the centuries, they are clearly and unequivocally in direct contradiction with the very essence of Christianity itself. You're probably aware that all of the big, horrible things that have been done over the years were done when Christianity was an "official religion." Oh man, what a gigantic, indeed even eternal, mistake it was to turn Christianity into a state religion. Many say that one of the most tragic days in history was when Constantine established Christianity as the official religion of the Roman Empire. Christianity, as I said in one of my very first letters, is not a political religion! It's a relationship with the true, living God of the universe bound in truth, justice and love (and the American way, heh heh...oh wait that's Superman). As soon as it became wedded to the state, it ceased being "Christian". I really can't stress that enough. The black stain of the Crusades, of the Inquisition, of the "conversion" of the New World has reverberated throughout the centuries and is still powerfully with us even today, as evidenced by the fact that I'm sitting here writing about it. But Jordan, please please please don't throw the baby out with the bathwater. If you're going to reject Christianity, at least know what it is you're rejecting. Reject Jesus, not Christianity. Heck, even I reject Christianity as a religion, because THAT'S NOT WHAT IT IS.

Here's some quotes from *Church History in Plain Language* by Bruce L. Shelley that aptly describe this situation:

> *How can the church employ violence to safeguard a peaceful society? The church deliberately accepted a line of action all but impossible to reconcile with the eternal kingdom toward which she aspired. She created the Inquisition, no only to execute heretics but to subject them to deliberate and prolonged torture. In driving out one devil the church opened the door for seven others....The infamy of this institution has left its mark on the memories and vocabularies of men everywhere. We equate it with the ruthless miscarriage of justice....Unfortunately the popes never held two basic truths that we must never forget: Christianity's highest satisfactions are not guaranteed by possession of special places [i.e., the Crusades], and the sword is never God's way to extend Christ's church. This fault assured the religious collapse of the whole structure."* [7]

Think about it this way. Suppose you were able to attract 8 or 10 guys to you who believed what you said about spirituality. You all met regularly, and you were their 'leader', telling them about your feelings on 'God' and spirituality. Then suppose that a couple weeks later, for whatever reason, they went on a rampage, torturing people, burning others at the stake, and killing others with the sword, all the while claiming they were "doing it for the glory of Jordan and his beliefs." "In the name of Jordan, we kill you, unbeliever," they cried. What would happen? The news would get ahold of it, and suddenly you and your teachings would be reviled and despised. And what would you say? "Wait a minute! I never told those guys to do that! Don't blame me or my teachings. In fact my teachings say just the opposite—love everyone and be tolerant!" That's exactly what has happened in the history of the church. Yes, some horrible things were done, yes some terrible pains and sufferings were inflicted on many people, but…JESUS HAD NOTHING TO DO WITH IT. People used His Name, but his reality had nothing at all to do with it. You would want people to judge you based on the real you if the above situation occurred, and I'm pleading with you to give Jesus the same courtesy. Before you reject what he said, discover the real Him. Read the Gospel of Luke or Mark by yourself and with an open mind—without any preconceived notions either way, without any stereotypes in mind. Read about what he said and who he was <u>for yourself</u>. Only when you've done that, without any church telling you what he said and without any skeptic dismissing what he said and without any Inquisitor corrupting what he said, will you be qualified to make a judgment about him. I think you would like what you saw. Jesus was a progressive, too, just like you are. He was so 'progressive' that he scandalized the 'right-wing conservatives' of his day. He talked to women as people—which in those days was huge, He went to dinner with the social scum, he physically touched horribly diseased people (WAY against the Jewish rules of the day). People called him a drunk and a glutton because he loved to drink and eat and laugh with the 'sinners'. I think you'll be surprised if you take a fresh look at him…

Also remember that many of the world's highest goods came from the church as well. Science, hospitals, Mother Teresa, Abraham Lincoln, Dietrich Bonhoeffer, William Wilberforce, missions of mercy, caring for the needy (which is in contrast to the Eastern beliefs which teach that helping out a beggar ultimately harms him because it's delaying the payment of his karmic debt), all these and more came out of the church. And even when the church was doing evil things, not ALL the church was hopelessly evil. In each of those instances, there was always a counter-movement of Christians horrified at the abuses of the church and speaking out against it. Unfortunately, they didn't control the microphone so their message didn't get broadcast very loudly. So she (the church) was never ALL bad, let's not forget that.

One final, sad note before moving on. You know, we condemn ourselves whenever we talk about how 'evil' the Europeans were when they came over here to conquer the Native Americans. We condemn ourselves because we enjoy the benefits of what they did while at the same time spitting with disgust and calling them inhumane monsters. If we were truly honest with ourselves I think that we'd admit to being glad on some level that it happened. And if we were truly repulsed with all our heart at what they did, and truly interested in justice for the wronged, we would give this land back to those from whom our ancestors stole it from. I know that I personally am not willing to do that, and I am disgusted with myself for feeling that way—all I can do is ask God to forgive my wicked, selfish heart.

Okay, here comes a big challenge…hell. Not a comfortable thing to think about, imagine, or talk about. This is the part of the letter that'll take the longest to write, as I sit here and reflect myself on what to say. I'll start by saying a few things. First, it's obvious that you've had some pretty bad experiences with Christianity in your past, especially in this area. I'm really sorry that that happened. Maybe you could tell me a little bit more about that part of your life. And please consider once again that whatever bad experience you had was not representative of Jesus. Second, let me just iterate this point again—we should not base our decisions about what is true and what we will live by on whether it makes us uncomfortable. Sometimes being uncomfortable can save your life. And sometimes being afraid can save your life, too. Finally, please read all this in the spirit in which it was conceived and written—one of sensitivity.

Before we get into the meat of this, I've got to call your attention to the fact that you've based your entire view of this subject on a grossly simplified stereotype of the concept of hell, and an almost cartoonish view of how it is preached. In point of fact, it is exceedingly rare to go to a church in America these days and even hear the word 'hell' mentioned, much less preached on. I'm not denying your experience—perhaps you used to go to a church that promulgated these stereotypes. If so, I can certainly understand how you would come to detest the very idea as you do now. All I can say is please reopen your mind to the possibility that hell exists, in spite of the shoddy foundation that was laid in your heart by some perhaps well-meaning but nonetheless destructive words.

> *"Hell is God's great compliment to the reality of human freedom and the dignity of human choice."* —G.K. Chesterton

That quote is pretty much it in a nutshell. Let me attempt, in all humility, to explore the issue in a bit more detail. I'm going to rely heavily on others' work, as I couldn't really say anything better or fuller than what others already have. Here we go. What is hell? Perhaps we should start by saying what it is not. First, hell is not "the fire and burning thing."

That is symbolism. The metaphor of fire merely points the way to the reality. After all, how could hell literally be filled with fire when Jesus also describes hell as "outer darkness"? Hell is not a torture chamber. This is not to mitigate the horror of hell, just to clarify it a bit. And by the way, Jesus talked more about hell than anyone else in the Bible. Just about everything we know about it comes from Him. You might say that He was mistaken on this issue or something, but I think the reason He talked about it so much was that He desperately wants no one to end up there. *"God did not send His Son into the world to condemn the world, but to save the world through Him"* (Jn 3:17). If you're in danger of driving over a cliff, the loving thing to do is warn you about it. "To say that anyone who teaches and warns about hell is immoral is like saying that any mother who warns her children not to play with fire is immoral. It is just plain silly." [8]

Another thing hell is not is a place that God angrily throws people who don't worship "in a certain way." Once again, that's a 'religious' way of looking at hell. God is not religious. He is real. He is relational. He is not religious. Religion is man's externalizing and ritualizing the spirit. Religion is mankind coming up with a bunch of different ways to please God and gain His acceptance. If you think about God as a reality, as a real living Being, rather than a religious idea or feeling, it helps you understand this much better. That being said, I think when you come at the issue of hell as "the place God condemns you to for not worshipping His way," I think you're coming from the wrong angle. The Bible makes this quite clear: *"I take no pleasure in the death of the wicked"* (Ezekiel 33:11), and *"He is patient with you, not wanting anyone to perish, but everyone to come to repentance"* (2 Pe 3:9). It is also clear that if a person "goes to God with a yearning, passionate, innocent, loving heart," as you stated, then they will ultimately make it into heaven. This is not to say that one can make it into heaven without Jesus, but that one whose heart is truly in the place that you described (and I would add a lover of truth) then God will either make them aware of Jesus somehow, or He will apply what Jesus has done for them even though they may never have heard of Him. The problem is that most people don't have yearning, passionate, innocent, and loving hearts. A lot of people say they do, but if you show them the truth about God in a gentle, loving, and respectful way, you soon see that they are not sincere in saying that. Many, many people don't truly want to know the real, living God; they want a boxed and prepackaged god that agrees with them, helps them feel better about themselves, and never, EVER makes demands on them or (God forbid!) says that they're not living right. This applies to many people who call themselves Christians, as well. So, back on the topic—God does not send people to hell. People send themselves there, through a lifetime of refusing God, stubbornly resisting repentance, and refusing to give up their own pride. As theologian D.A. Carson says:

> *Hell is not a place where people are consigned because they were pretty good blokes, but they just didn't believe the right stuff. They're consigned there, first and foremost, because they defy their maker and want to be at the center of the universe. Hell is not filled with people who have already repented, only God isn't gentle enough or good enough to let them out. It's filled with people who, for all eternity, still want to be the center of the universe and who persist in their God-defying rebellion.*
>
> *What is God to do? If he says it doesn't matter to him, then God is no longer a God to be admired. He's either amoral or positively creepy. For him to act in any other way in the face of such blatant defiance would be to reduce God himself.* [9]

That quote brings me to the first thing that hell is. Hell is necessary. In a world where free will exists, there must exist the possibility of a hell. Free will involves the possibility that some will freely choose to rebel against God and try to set themselves up as their own god, in many ways. God could not possibly force us all to go to heaven. You see, He values love above all else in existence, as you rightly have intuited. But what is love if it is forced upon you? Whatever it is, it is not love. By its very definition, love is an act of the will. So in a world of free will, you can be certain that some will refuse that love (I talked a little about that in a previous letter). What is hell but the only alternative to a life lived in opposition to God? After all, for one whose supreme desire is to be the center of the universe, Heaven would be hell for them. For the greatest virtues in Heaven will be humility, adoration of another (God), giving rather than receiving, and sacrificial love.

Hell is also a total separation from God—physical, spiritual, and eternal. We really don't know very much concretely about hell beyond this. We know that no one in hell will enjoy it—it will be joyless and loveless because God _is_ joy and love, and to be separated from Him is to be separated from those—but everyone who ends up there will have chosen it, by the way they lived life. No one will be there by accident.

The fact that hell exists and is a horrible place does not rob God of his unconditional love. In fact, as the Chesterton quote points out, the existence of hell is God's supreme acknowledgement of the dignity of humankind and our ability to live freely. One author theorizes that the very fires of hell may be made of God's love, a self-sacrificial *agape* that mocks the sinner's love of egotism, pride, and self. A child throwing a temper tantrum in a fit of rage may feel tortured by his parent's hugs and kisses. Remember *Amadeus*? Mozart's music was so filled with divine beauty that it enraged Salieri, who was consumed by jealousy because he did not share the gift that had been given Mozart. So it may be that it is God's love itself, or rather the sinner's hatred of that love, that constitutes the pain of hell. Who knows?

When you contemplate hell, you must think about it in the proper context of everything else we know about God. Hell is not some isolated doctrine—it is part of the grand tapestry that God has created called reality. Is it hard? Yes. It shocks the mind and the emotions. But then, that can be a good thing, if the possibility of you going there shocks you awake enough to consider your standing with God. Is it complicated and complex? Yes. But then, isn't that true of everything that corresponds to reality? Another thing to remember is that we must also have an accurate portrait of hell before we reject it and call a God who would create such a place a monster. Hopefully I have done that in some small way here. I have tried not to be superficial in my treatment, but in a discussion this short there necessarily is much left out. For all the mistakes, unclarities, and lack of substance, I apologize. Much of my job in talking to people about God is clearing away the misconceptions, stereotypes, and prejudices people have. Most people love the real Jesus when they discover Him, but reject Christianity the "religion". I can understand that. After all, I too reject the Christian "religion" as does every true Christian on this planet. We're in good company—Jesus rejected religion, too. In my experience, no mere "religion" corresponds to reality. Only true Christianity does. True Christianity delivers us what we truly want the most—freedom, security, purpose, and love.

Finally, to close out the subject of hell that I very briefly touched on, let me ask the question again. What else do you want God to do? He has created us, made His existence known through the very existence of this amazing, miraculous universe, sent prophets to tell us what He is like and how we should respond, inspired people to write down things that eventually became known as the Bible (the authenticity of which I talked about in a previous letter), and finally, in the ultimate act of sacrificial love, came down Himself in the person of Jesus (Yeshua, technically), teaching us about His existence and His ways, then went to die for us so that we don't have to pay the consequence for our own rebellion! He has provided a wealth of evidence for us to believe in Him, if we so choose, but not so much that we are forced against our will to follow Him. After all, you're right, God doesn't want us to follow Him because we're afraid of Him, but because we love Him. So, in light of all that, what else do you want God to do?!? Some people just don't want anything to do with that. And like I (actually C.S. Lewis) said before, *"There are only two kinds of people in the end: those who say to God, 'Thy will be done,' and those to whom God says, in the end, 'Thy will be done.'"* [10]

Okay, as a presidential debate moderator would say: new topic. Let me touch exceedingly briefly on how you closed out your last letter: the topic of evolution. First, it is imperative that we define terms here. The word 'evolution' is so vague that we must clarify what we mean. First, there are two types of evolution: micro and macro. Everyone, even Christians, believes in microevolution. That's the stuff like Darwin's Galapagos turtles, Weiner's finch beak variations, dog breeding, etc. Microevolution is pretty much synonymous with adaptation, and no one disputes that this takes place. After all, it is directly observable. Macroevolution is different. Macroevolution is, according to the official Position Statement of the American National Association of Biology Teachers (quoted in Johnson, *Defeating Darwinism by Opening Minds*), as follows:

> *The diversity of life on earth is the outcome of evolution: an unsupervised, impersonal, unpredictable and natural process of temporal descent with genetic modification that is affected by natural selection, chance, historical contingencies and changing environments."* (You obviously don't believe in this completely, at least not the 'unsupervised' part, because you believe in some sort of Divine, but I'll deal with this definition because the things I'll bring up also cover theistic evolution.)

Macroevolution doesn't deal with dog breeding, etc. It deals with how dogs came to be in the first place. This is the evolution that tells us humans came from monkeys, birds came from dinosaurs, and every living thing in existence came from small, single-celled, bacteria-like organisms, which came from organic compounds floating in the early earth ocean, which came from exploding star matter, which came from the Big Bang, which ultimately and spontaneously came from…nothing at all!

So I absolutely must know what you mean when you talk about evolution before I can attempt a relevant response. But I'll just give a few things to think about. This idea of macroevolution is a theory in grave distress at the beginning of the 21st century. You wouldn't know it by reading the newspaper or listening to TV, because the scientists hold the microphone, and they've turned this evolution into a religion with no God. They are the leaders of this "religion" and are looked at as infallible in what they say by the general public; thus, they have a whole lot to lose in abandoning this theory. But abandon it they must, eventually, because it's a theory that doesn't hold water. Much, MUCH more could be said, and perhaps we can talk more about it later, but here's a few basics:

Darwin himself said that the truth of his theory would be borne out or shown to be false by the fossil record. It's been over a century since he first proposed the theory, and we've collected hundreds of thousands of fossils since then. Guess what? The fossil record shows absolutely no evidence of macroevolution at all! Not one single transitional fossil has ever been found (i.e., an animal in the process of becoming another type of animal). All the fossils we have are type-complete, meaning they are completely bird, completely fish, completely reptile, not part reptile and part bird, and what have you. This is even more so the case in the area of the fossil record that is the most plentiful—marine invertebrates. If the theory were true, then there should be ample evidence of macroevolutionary change taking place on that level; however, it is conspicuously absent. Here's a quote from Niles Eldredge, one of the leading experts in the world on invertebrate fossils:

> *No wonder paleontologists shied away from evolution for so long. It never seems to happen. Assiduous collecting up cliff faces yields zigzags, minor oscillations, and the very occasional slight accumulation of change—over millions of years, at a rate too slow to account for all the prodigious change that has occurred in evolutionary history. When we do see the introduction of evolutionary novelty, it usually shows up with a bang, and often with no firm evidence that the fossils did not evolve elsewhere! Evolution cannot forever be going on somewhere else. Yet that's how the fossil record has struck many a forlorn paleontologist looking to learn something about evolution.* [11]

This brings up another point: the Cambrian explosion. The fossil record shows that, sometime in the Cambrian period, all of the basic animal groups show up suddenly, all at once, and without any evidence of evolutionary ancestry. Pop! They're just suddenly there! Scientists are still trying to explain it away.

And of course, there's the massive problem of all the matter in the universe just suddenly springing into being out of nothing. That's something that so defies common sense (and well-established, observable laws of science) that it takes more faith to believe that this happened than to believe in an infinite Being who has the power to create us.

The second law of thermodynamics states that all the energy in the universe is running down and providing less and less useful work. It's called the law of entropy and is one of the most firmly established laws of science that there is. Basically, it says that everything in the universe is winding down, to less and less orders of complexity. Macroevolution runs in direct contradiction to this law of science. It states that matter is ordering itself, randomly and with no help, into higher and higher levels of complexity. Scientists try to justify it in a number of ways, like saying there are pockets in the universe where order is increasing, and pockets where it is decreasing by the same amount, so that everything evens out. There is, however, no observable evidence to support this at all. It is a blind-faith proposition. You are right in saying that "science doesn't start with a notion/theory and...try to force-fit everything into that parameter conveniently leaving out or ignoring the results that don't quite jibe with the original hypothesis." You are right. <u>Science</u> doesn't do that, but you are quite naïve if you believe that scientISTS don't do that. Like I said, they have a lot to lose by admitting that there is no hard evidence for macroevolution. They are being forced to come up with increasingly ridiculous and un-scientific theories to hold on to their theory, such as "punctuated equilibrium", where a new animal type suddenly emerges, fully formed out of the egg of another type (e.g., a bird popping out of a snake egg), and even space-seeding by UFO's! Some scientists are actually considering this!

Common sense tells us this universe has a Designer. When you're walking through a forest and you spot a wristwatch on the path, you know that this watch was designed by someone in some factory somewhere. You know this because it exhibits hallmarks of design: order, complexity, and function. Now look at the universe, look at the human body, look at the single cell! These things are more ordered, complex, and purposeful than anything that the wildest imaginations of our brightest scientists could come up with. If something as lowly as a wristwatch compels us to assume it had a designer, how on earth can we then go on to say about the universe: "Enh. Happened by chance." Please.

This sort of brings up the anthropic principle. This says that everything in this universe is precisely tuned to be able to support life here on this planet. There are about a hundred or so parameters, that we know of thus far, which, if any one of them were different in the smallest degree (we're talking less than 1% here), life would be utterly impossible here on earth. The distance of the earth to the sun, distance of the moon, size of the moon, size of the earth, size of the sun, axial tilt of the earth, rotation period of earth, chemicals in earth's atmosphere, freezing properties of water (Water freezes top-down, in contrast to every other liquid which freezes bottom-up. If that were the case with water, life would be impossible), the force of gravity, the position of the other planets in our solar system, size of our galaxy, relationship of our galaxy to the other galaxies near it, relationship of those galaxies to all the other galaxies in the universe, it all comes together ABSOLUTELY PRECISELY in order to have life here on this planet. Almost as if the universe was designed that way...

Irreducible complexity is another issue that's just come up in the past 5 years or so. Once we were able to look inside cells and begin to understand how they work, we saw how incredibly complex every single one of them was, much more than the blob of slime that scientists in Darwin's day thought them to be. Irreducible complexity states that there are many structures in living cells and organisms that must have every piece of it present and in working order before the mechanism as a whole can work. You can't slowly build upon the eye, adding a piece here and there over the eons, and come up with an eye. If just the smallest piece of the eye was missing, the entire thing would not work. It is irreducibly complex. There are many other structures considered to be irreducibly complex.

Like I said, I'm not sure just exactly what kind of evolution you're talking about, but there are some of the gaping holes in the theory of macroevolution. One other thing, and I mean this in all sensitivity. Your view of evolution, Jordan, is seriously romanticized. Evolution is not brilliant and graceful, and it certainly does not prove a loving God's existence. Evolution is messy, unpredictable, random, and exceedingly brutal. Truly "red in tooth and claw," as Tennyson would put it. How in the world can you reconcile survival of the fittest and death for the weak with your view of a loving God-force, Jordan? Luckily we don't have to, though the ones holding the microphone would like us to think we do. Don't you realize that with Darwinian evolution as your framework, right and wrong is relegated to what will help you survive better, even and especially if it means destroying those weaker than you? What do you think was the moral/philosophical underpinning of the Nazi Holocaust/Master Race?

Here are some quotes form Darwin:

> *The more civilized so-called Caucasian races have beaten the Turkish hollow in the struggle for existence. Looking to the world at no very distant date, what an endless number of the lower races will have been eliminated by the higher civilized races throughout the world.* [12]

> *At some future period, not very distant as measured by centuries, the civilized races of man will almost certainly exterminate, and replace, the savage races throughout the world.* [13]

and one from Thomas Huxley, nicknamed "Darwin's bulldog":

> *No rational man, cognizant of the facts, believes that the average Negro is the equal, still less the superior, of the white man....It is simply incredible that...he will be able to compete successfully with his bigger-brained and smaller-jawed rival, in a contest which is to be carried on by thoughts and not by bites.* [14]

Ouch. 'Nuf said.

Oh man. I said I was going to be exceedingly brief. What an utter failure! =) So now I'll finally wrap up. I think I've said this before, but it bears repeating. I've talked about a lot of stuff here, trying to show you that Christianity is rational, and indeed real. It's all important stuff, too, especially to one who has objections to these issues. But ultimately these are all secondary issues which must take second place to the prime issue—the Resurrection of Jesus. For without that, all this is meaningless. So what if I've shown that it's rational, even loving, to believe in hell, if you don't believe that Jesus rose from the dead? Because if that didn't happen, then the whole edifice of Christianity crumbles into mere philosophy, religion and "believe it if it works for you." The whole reason I write these letters in defense of the Christian faith (I don't like the word 'defense'—I think the case in favor of Christianity is so strong that its opponents are the ones who should be 'defending', but Christianity is the one being attacked all the time, so it is appropriate) is so that you'll perhaps consider once more in your life that Jesus lived, died, and rose again from the dead for YOU, Jordan, and wants to be in a relationship with you, as He is with me. All paths that include a look at Jesus must intersect at the empty tomb, for without it, all of Christianity, and I would contend, all of life, is ultimately meaningless. If you are to be honest, you <u>must</u> deal with that and not dismiss it with a shrug of the shoulders. For if it happened, it is literally the most important event in all of human history. And if it really did happen, then it will one day become the most important single thing in your life, one way or the other. Something that serious deserves to be looked at with the utmost sincerity and honesty. You owe it to yourself, Jordan.

I also, like you, feel something well up inside me as I write these words, and perhaps you think me a fool for believing in "fairy tales and medieval myths," but it takes a lot of courage for me to say these things, because I open myself up to vitriolic and irrational attacks whenever I do. I know it took a lot of courage for you to reject religion, as you said. I applaud your bravery to do that; I only ask that you don't reject the Jesus who rejected religion along with you. At least not until you've given Him your time and some serious reflection and meditation.

The other reason that it scares me to talk about these things with others is that I know that I don't live up to the ideals that Jesus preached. Every day I fall short of what I'm capable of and what I should be. Heck, you've observed me do that. I curse, gossip, get angry, and all kinds of things right in front of the guy who I'm telling about Jesus and how wonderful Christianity is. I try real hard to be a great example and a good person, but I ain't perfect and I shudder with profound horror at the thought that my actions as a professed follower of Jesus may turn someone off to His message. All I hope for is that someone would look at me, look at my life, and say, "Maybe this Jesus guy isn't all that bad." I want Jesus to be proud of me, to be proud to send me to tell others about Him. Sometimes He isn't. But He's always there to forgive me, pick me up and dust me off when I look to Him again. I'd hate to see what sort of person I'd become without the grace of God. Actually, I can get a glimpse of it. During the times when I'm not in tune with Him, I get a glimpse of what my life would be like 24/7 without Him at all, and let me tell you it sucks big time! So yes, it scares me, but the potential benefits far outweigh the risks. I get to play a part in helping someone come into a relationship with God and see their life take on new meaning, purpose, and perspective! I think if you asked Monica, though she's been fortunate to lead a pretty charmed life, she would tell you that she's better off now than before she knew God.

Man this was long, but you brought up some pretty big issues, so it's your fault! =) I'll go now. Thanks again for this correspondence. It's awesome.

Blessings,

Jeremy

Truth poorly defended loses not it truthfulness;
likewise Falsehood aptly defended loses not its falsity.

Sent: Thursday, November 9, 2000
Subject: Deep, but short thoughts

Wow! Mr. Seely. Every time I think I have this correspondence wrapped up, like the election imbroglio, one layer peeled only reveals another deeper, more meaningful layer, and I quite enjoyably get to view this deep man called Jeremy Seely.

There are so many areas I want to comment on in your last letter. First let me say we have a lot, and I mean *a lot* of convergence. We have more than I thought. I was surprised and I think you may be too. I'm going to write in paragraphed chunks here to try to get to everything. It probably won't be in order of importance, I'll be writing as it flows to me.

I'm going to blow your mind right now with the first bit of news. Jesus has been my friend for a long, long time. I have walked with Jesus for many years. Surprised? I thought you would be. Many people perceive me to not know him. Fundys (thank you for that term, it helps with brevity, and I don't put you in that category unless you like it) assume that "metaphysical people" have no relationship with Jesus. It couldn't be further from the truth with many, many people in the New Thought movement.

Here's an example:
Much like I assumed you would be voting for Bush and was deeply humbled and embarrassed when you showed me yet another layer of yourself (revealing your environmental concerns), many fundys assume they too, have a monopoly on truth. When you revealed your vote to me, it was revealing for me of my prejudice, judgments, and yet another example for me of how I fall so very short of my spiritual heritage. Thank you for reminding me to at least try to not judge. I thank you for your continually opening your mind to all the ways God is continually reminding you as well. I know too we will both fall short in our attempts to be all-envisioning with each other :)

OK, back to the big one which is probably where your attention stuck anyway :> My walk with Jesus. Let me reveal some of my communications: In Eastern or New Thought we stress much more importance on the listening to God than the talking to God. A common saying is God gave us two ears and one mouth and wants us to use them accordingly. This is why we put such emphasis on meditation. We too believe in prayer, and know that God stands at the ready to answer. But there is more emphasis on reflection.

> *Yes, some horrible things were done, yes some terrible pains and sufferings were inflicted on many people, but...JESUS HAD NOTHING TO DO WITH IT. People used His Name, but his reality had nothing at all to do with it. You would want people to judge you based on the real you if the above situation occurred, and I'm pleading with you to give Jesus the same courtesy. Before you reject what he said, discover the real Him. Read the Gospel of Luke, or Mark, by yourself and with an open mind—without any preconceived notions either way, without any stereotypes in mind. Read about what he said and who he was for yourself. Only when you've done that, without any church telling you what he said and without any skeptic dismissing what he said and without any Inquisitor corrupting what he said, will you be qualified to make a judgment about him. I think you would like what you saw. Jesus was a progressive, too, just like you are. He was so 'progressive' that he scandalized the 'right-wing conservatives' of his day. He talked to women as people—which in those days was huge, He went to dinner with the social scum, he physically touched horribly diseased people (WAY against the Jewish rules of the day). People called him a drunk*

and a glutton because he loved to drink and eat and laugh with the 'sinners'. I think you'll be surprised if you take a fresh look at him...

Also remember that many of the world's highest goods came from the church as well. Science, hospitals, Mother Teresa, Abraham Lincoln, Dietrich Bonhoeffer, William Wilberforce, missions of mercy, caring for the needy (which is in contrast to the Eastern beliefs which teach that helping out a beggar ultimately harms him because it's delaying the payment of his karmic debt), all these and more came out of the church. And even when the church was doing evil things, not ALL the church was hopelessly evil. In each of those instances, there was always a counter-movement of Christians horrified at the abuses of the church and speaking out against it. Unfortunately, they didn't control the microphone so their message didn't get broadcast very loudly. So she (the church) was never ALL bad, let's not forget that.

Oh my God! (well we're talking 'bout him aren't we?) This is so cool that you mentioned these things. I am in complete harmony with everything in these two paragraphs except one. First the things I agree on: The misunderstanding of Jesus' words are the very crux of so many, many problems we have today. Don't forget that we live in a heavily populated country of people who consider themselves followers of Christ. I have been exposed (who in this country hasn't?) to the writings of those books you mentioned. It was some of the quotes from those books and my meditations that allowed me to open my heart to Jesus. I also love all those people you mentioned who quite clearly draw their strength from Christ. The one sentence in there that I don't agree with is your interpretation of Karmic debt. The truly "enlightened" in the east actually choose the life of a beggar. In India for example, even if one was from the highest caste and could look forward to a life of luxury, if he or she was a true believer, would renounce all worldly possessions and choose the life of a renounceiate. These life-long "beggars" are seen in the east as great Masters, and the general citizenry squabbles over who gets to bathe them and take them into their homes.

One final, sad note before moving on. You know, we condemn ourselves whenever we talk about how 'evil' the Europeans were when they came over here to conquer the Native Americans. We condemn ourselves because we enjoy the benefits of what they did while at the same time spitting with disgust and calling them inhumane monsters. If we were truly honest with ourselves I think that we'd admit to being glad on some level that it happened. And if we were truly repulsed with all our heart at what they did, and truly interested in justice for the wronged, we would give this land back to those from whom our ancestors stole it from. I know that I personally am not willing to do that, and I am disgusted with myself for feeling that way—all I can do is ask

> *God to forgive my wicked, selfish heart.*

How eloquent Sir. I fully agree

> *The other point is that, whatever the reasons for all the evils that have been done in the name of Christ over the centuries, they are clearly and unequivocally in direct contradiction with the very essence of Christianity itself.*

I would take point with this. The very essence of "Christianity" if I am to understand what so many fundys tell me, is: "*ours* is the way the *only* way."

This concept of "*ours* is the *only* way" is the very crux of all the evils done, and done unfortunately in the name of Christ. So you started that paragraph with "*whatever the reasons for all the evils done.*" Here's the reasons: The institutionalization of a man called Christ, then through that institutionalization of Christ, claiming a monopoly on truth. It is in this very "staking of the claim" that the permission for evil is granted.

> *My point here is that it seems to me that you're equating all religious certainty with oppression, and I'm just saying that even though it has happened with Christianity in the past and with other religions in the present, you can't use that as an argument against religious certainty in itself, because the two are not logically related.*

It has happened with Christianity in the past and is happening with Christianity right now. It's happening with other religions as well. So whether they're logically related or not, this it the result. Whether it's Christians persecuting Muslims in Bosnia, Muslims persecuting Hindus in Pakistan, Jews persecuting Muslims in Palestine, Hindus persecuting Christians in India, it's all wrong, and it's all a *direct* result of religious certainty. It is a direct result of dogma.

It's not God's plan. The slaughtering over "path" is a *direct result* of the staking of "the claim." God weeps and nods his head as I am guided to tell my beloved brother this.

> *God is not religious. He is real. He is relational. He is not religious. Religion is man's externalizing and ritualizing the spirit. Religion is mankind coming up with a bunch of different ways to please God and gain His acceptance. If you think about God as a reality, as a real living Being, rather than a religious idea or feeling, it helps you understand this much better.*

I think you're on to something there. I like it baby!

I'm getting glassy eyed so for now, I will quit.

I know I didn't answer all your inquiries, which in a way can be thought of as a Tao answer. To be in Zen, or of the Tao, I would immediately not answer or say one word to your thoughtful inquiries. I would just love you deeply, for that is the connection with God, which in my book is, and will always be, much more of an answer than any of our mental gymnastics and interpretations.

I must confess though, I don't have the discipline to not respond. It's too much fun!!

More later
Blessings!

☙❧

Sent: Thursday, November 9, 2000
Subject: addendum

You are in my thoughts. Would you be open to listening to a tape? It's intense, by a man called Allen Watts. An IQ of 175+

Chock full of Biblical reference, and fully explains the Buddhist's take on Christ and religion.

☙❧

Sent: Saturday, November 11, 2000
Subject: Yes

Sure, I would love to listen to it. I'm always up for that kind of thing, as I think you know by now!

There's a book out there that I've been meaning to check out called *Living Buddha/Living Christ.* Have you heard of it or read it? It sounds like it might be similar to what this Allen Watts guy is talking about
.

Sent: Sunday, November 12, 2000
Subject: Re: Yes

Living Buddha/Living Christ is excellent. I had the tape series for a while, lent it out and unfortunately, lost track of it.

I have heard, but cannot confirm, that Christians like it. I just remember it being a wonderful bringing together of thought and culture. I would love to peruse your material as well. Tapes are usually better for me as a lot of my time is spent in my car. I also have quite a few books I'm reading currently, so it wouldn't be til June or July that I could get to it! So tapes are the best!

One of the books I'm reading now is absolutely blowing my mind. It's called *Friendship with God* by Neale Donald Walsch. Every single page enriches and deepens my love and understanding of God. I give it two very enthusiastic thumbs up!

On the Alan Watts tape, I would want to talk to you before you listen. Mr. Watts has some very harsh words for Christian/Religion, but that in no way has anything to do with his love for Jesus. Just take what you want and leave what you don't. I feel confident there will be at least a couple of places where you will think to yourself *"Wow! I never thought of that!"* Of course, that's just my projection, you may hate it!

Enjoying this correspondence

Sent: Saturday, November 25, 2000
Subject: (no subject)

Jordan,

Thanks for the last letter. We *do* have much agreement on many important issues. That's great! Hopefully our agreements are bound in truth, because otherwise they don't amount to much. After all, many thousands of Nazis were in agreement with each other as well!

Perhaps we're both partially right in our view of karma and karmic debt. It may be true, I must confess that I don't know for certain, that the true Hindus strove to be beggars. But practically, one of the reasons that the caste system was so oppressive and unjust was because it relied on the law of karma to uphold it. The station you were born into was ironclad, and you couldn't break out of it. You were there for a reason—your past lives. It's just like what we've been saying about Christianity. True Christians didn't oppress, enslave and murder unbelievers, but practically, Christianity *was* used as a justification for such acts—whether it was rational or not.

I am aware and do understand that a true Tao/Zen answer would be to not answer anything I've brought up. Yes, love *is* more important than debate. But to me that line of approach also sounds like something else...a copout. To be blunt, it sounds very much like, "Don't bother me with the facts, I've already made up my mind." Even a Zen Buddhist looks both ways before crossing the street. Meditate on that for a few minutes and I think you'll understand what I'm saying.

I think it's awesome that you consider Jesus your friend! You've walked with him for many years—tell me about him! I'd like to know!

Blessings,

Jeremy

Sent: Monday, November 27, 2000
Subject: Re: (no subject)

Jeremy thank you for the wonderful letter. I want you to know that I'm going to try to get to it tonight. Just wanted to immediately thank you for your thoughtfulness.

Sent: Monday, November 27, 2000
Subject: Re: Re: (no subject)

Same to you bro.

Hope you had a great Thanksgiving with your family and/or friends!

Love,

J

Sent: Monday, November 27, 2000
Subject: Rather lengthy reply!! :)

Hey Buddy,

I'm a bit exhausted after the Dentist drilled in my head for many hours today, and lots of LA smog, but I'm also feeling a weird sense of energy to write you at the same time, an interesting juxtaposition indeed.

Let me first say I **really** feel an increasing appreciation for our dialogue, and you as a friend. It's so nice to experience a true give and take with a curious student and teacher. Your curiosity and thirst for theological knowledge and understanding is to me, a testament to the living spirit inside you, so very hungry to express, and get closer and closer to God. I'm just flat out happy to have you as a pen pal and theatrical colleague.

Let me address your last letter (which was a bit shorter than your usual :>)

I am totally on the same page with you about what the Hindus did and do to their people. Just as horrific as Christians, Muslims, and Jews do to their "others"...I am by no means justifying or excusing their bad acts just because they happen to believe in many paths to God. Bad acts are bad acts period. I know we both agree on that.

I am now going to go deeply into my spiritual faith in this and many following letters. I've pretty much told you I don't believe in only one path to God. I believe as many grains of sand as are on this planet times infinity twice is the amount of ways to introduce yourself to, then get to know, then continually converse with, then develop friendship with, then communion with God. So put on your seat belt!! If this deepens your understanding of my friendship with God, yowsa!! If not, I hope it at least makes for good reading ;)

When I was a kid, a good chunk of my family was Catholic. The amount of ritual and fear swirling around God was staggering. An odd mixture of God loves you so much you can't even know!, and make sure you love God this way or you will burn in hell for eternity. This used to scare the shit out of me. I could not reconcile a God who knew my heart and loved me unconditionally with this 'God loves you if' statement. Even as a four year old my instincts told me God had to be one or the other. He was either so big and so unconditional or he was conditional and I had to love him a certain way. As I grow in my knowledge and love for God, I now realize my innocence and instincts were right on. God never puts a condition on his infinite love (matter o' fact you cannot have a condition on infinite love, see the contradiction in terms? An absolute impossibility to have both). Jeremy, think about it...Let me demonstrate:

We've talked about projection...
For thousands of years we've projected a God of conditions. We say God wants you to love him. We say his love is infinite so he doesn't need

anything and would never force us to love him. Then in the same breath we say if we don't love him a certain way, he will brutally punish us for eternity. I say that is our measly little projection of him as a jealous, guarded, greedy, nervous little entity. I assure you he is none of these. When I show you why, it will blow your mind, and it will allow you to love him more deeply and thoroughly than you ever dreamed in your wildest imagination. Also, one of the nice residual effects will be to truly love mankind unconditionally as well. For you see, this limited, unfair, unreasonable projection we have of God as all of those negative traits I explained earlier, is what gives us an excuse to love our fellow mankind conditionally as well. "For what's good enough for God must be good enough for us." When you have revelation of the depths to which we've sunken in our appraisal of the infinite, it's humbling to say the least. OK, let's take some categories to explore:

Is there only one faith that can lay claim to the truth?
All religions with the possible exception of Buddhism have tried very hard to co-opt God's love and be sole owner of it.
Kinda like trying to scoop up the ocean with three spoons and say "I have it all." Each religion says God loves us and only us cuz we have the answer. We are the chosen people. We are the one true church! These religions are very jealous of the standing they've bestowed upon themselves. If someone then says "Hey God's love is *bigger* than that! God embraces all faiths, all nations, all people," these churches that claim monopoly on God's love call that blasphemy. Most religions claim that they say God gives freedom to make the choice, but then go on to say you will be tortured endlessly and damned eternally for making a choice God didn't want you to make. Under this logic God didn't give you freedom to make any choice, he gave you ability. But you are not free under this logic, not if you care about the outcome.

So, this is how we have it constructed under the last two thousand years of religion: If God is to grant you your reward in heaven, God expects you to do things his way. This, you call God's unconditional love. Then we hold each other in this same place of expectation and call this *love*. Yet it is not love, in either case, *it is a trade*! which is not love! for love expects nothing save what freedom provides, and freedom knows nothing of expectation.

God does not have Neediness, God does not have Expectation, and God does not have Jealousy. Any of these traits denotes less than perfect love. We cannot truly love each other when any of these traits are present, and we certainly can't love a God who indulges in any of these, much less all of them. Yet that is exactly the kind of God we believe in, and since we've declared it good enough for God......These projections are deeply embedded in our psyche it will take a major undertaking to root them out. Until we do, we can never truly love one another, much less God.

To increase our ability to receive God's abundant love, we must raise our awareness of how big and infinite God is, so that we don't project limits on God's love, for we can only receive God's love in the way that we *give* our love to God. Thus, you have the true reciprocal relationship.

More later my friend.............

ಸಿಂಡ

Sent: Sunday, December 3, 2000
Subject: Addendum

Hey Buddy,

It was great seeing you last night. Isn't it fun to have fun no matter what's going on around you? Some people enrolled in "this is a drag because they're not listening to us" but I just stayed in "We'll win them back, or we won't, but I'm having fun, practice, and fellowship with my loved ones, what an honor!"

So, I'm very curious to hear your feedback on some of my postulations. I hope I answered your questions. If I didn't answer them to your satisfaction, please specify so I can try to be more specific. In the meantime, I would like to ask you a few more to try to understand your Theology.

If you don't want to answer any of these, that's cool, these just came to me in my meditations.

1. Do you believe we are separate from God?

2. Do you believe a child or a newborn is fundamentally wrong or sinned until he or she performs something a certain way?

3. Do you believe in conditionality?

4. Do you believe heaven is somewhere else?

5. Do you believe that there is hell?

6. Do you believe that God judges?

7. Do you believe that God's love is conditional?

8. Do you believe that you need anything?

9. Do you believe you create your own reality?

10. Do you believe there is such a thing as punishment?

೧೦೦೩

Sent: Wednesday, December 6, 2000
Subject: Re: Your letter

Hey there bud,

I also feel an increasing appreciation of the gift God has given us—this opportunity to talk at length about these things. It is a privilege and an honor! I know you get teased a lot about being superficial, but these letters show that, in the spiritual realm, you have done much asking, meditating, and listening in your search for truth. Ah well, maybe you *do* have an interesting view on women (heh heh) but in the spiritual arena you are far more profound than most of the people I know, even if I do disagree with you on a few crucial issues.

I begin to get a sense of your spiritual roots as you tell me about your upbringing. For good or for bad, our upbringing lays a groundwork that shapes our views for the rest of our lives—a groundwork that is very difficult to alter once set. I begin to see, at least partially, where your vehement disdain for certain aspects of "religion" come from when you tell me about the details of your Catholic background, and you would probably understand me a bit better by knowing that I come from a pretty solid Christian background (in the good sense!).

I can totally understand why you felt so instinctually at odds with the things you were being exposed to as a kid. If what you described was actually what was being taught (and in your perception, it *was*), then I would also feel in my spirit that it wasn't right. You are so right about God's love. He loves us infinitely and unconditionally! There is nothing you can do to make God love you any more or any less than He does at this very moment. That is absolutely, uncompromisingly, solid-as-a-rock True in my book (also in THE book—the Bible). But! The fact of God's unconditional love does not preclude out of hand the existence of the <u>biblical</u> definition of hell. I don't know if I was unclear in my last letter, or if you didn't read it quite carefully enough, or if your knee-jerk reaction to the very idea of hell prevented you from seeing what I was trying to communicate, but in my last letter I attempted to show, however briefly, how those two ideas can co-exist, and indeed must co-exist. What I attempted to describe was the biblical definition of hell, not the caricature that you were exposed to as a child and that

you now carry as part of your consciousness. I would urge you to read my last long letter again, because I think I did a pretty good job, albeit not definitive. That's just my opinion, though. I could have been totally abstruse =) Let me also add something else once more. You've said that you have a deep friendship with Jesus. Well, are you aware that He talked a whole lot about hell? He absolutely believed there was such a place, and He warned people to do anything at all to avoid ending up there. In fact, He said "if your right eye causes you to sin, gouge it out and throw it away. It is better for you to lose one part of your body than for your whole body to be thrown into hell." Matt 5:29
Something to meditate about…

Let me blow *your* mind now with something that's kind of related to this topic. Salvation. Christians say we are "saved," that we have received "salvation," a concept with which I'm sure you're familiar with. First of all, without going into any detail, let me just say that the biblical concept of salvation is much, much more than spiritual "fire insurance" or a "ticket to heaven." It entails salvation (wholeness) in this life as well. Here's the mind-blower: the Bible does not teach that only consciously-professing Christians will be saved! Did you know that? What the Bible teaches is that only Christ can save a person, but nowhere does it say that a person <u>absolutely must</u> have conscious, full-frontal-lobe-knowledge of Him for that to happen. If that were the case then people like Abraham and Moses would have been sent to hell too! This idea is explained so well in a book I have (*Handbook of Christian Apologetics*, by Kreeft and Tacelli, ch. 13) that anything I say beyond this would be mere plagiarism, so I think I'll make you a copy of the chapter and give it to you. You're right on that God is bigger than we can imagine, and that we often project our human frailties onto Him (e.g., the caricatures of hell, the caricature of God as an angry bully who throws you into 'the fiery pit' when He doesn't get His way, etc.). As the book that I just referenced says, God is truly "a bleeding-heart liberal." He desires everyone to be with him. There is only one way in the entire universe to thwart God's love…free will. The only person that can deflect God's love and salvation away from you is you. We can be confident that everyone on planet Earth <u>will</u> be "saved", except those who refuse such an awesome gift. I'm not here claiming to know who has or who hasn't been saved, how many or how few, how many Christians or how many non-Christians. I can't claim as Truth anything beyond what the Bible says, because it would be mere speculation. I do have my opinions, but that's what they are—opinions. Once again, this chapter in my book is so good (I think so anyway), please hold any criticisms of what I've just said until you've read it.

Here's a question you asked:

Is there only one faith that can lay claim to the truth?

Very early on in our correspondence I believe I answered that from my point of view, which hopefully is the Bible's POV as well. Let me answer again. First of all, all religions have some amount of truth in them. So if your question means "Is there only 1 faith that can lay claim to any truth?" I would answer no. But if the question means exactly what it says, "Is there 1 faith that can lay claim to THE truth?" I would answer yes. Not full and complete Truth, as only an infinite being can comprehend infinite truth, but the fullness of truth and the clearest expression of truth on our planet. I know that Christianity seems to be just one of many religions claiming to be the only way. But! Those claims are not for Christianity but for Christ. Christ is the one who claimed to be the only way, so if you have a problem with that you should take it up with him. And Christ is the only person with a legitimate reason for saying that. The foundation of Christianity is firmly rooted in space-time history, and as such can be historically verified or disproved. Religions such as Buddhism, etc. are principles of life and truth that can not be subjected to any kind of objective tests. People follow them because they were born into the faith, or because they like the teacher and the teachings. It feels good and true to them. Other of the so-called "historic" religions—Islam, Mormonism, etc.—have been demonstrated to be false, insofar as their sacred texts and beliefs can be verified historically. Sure, many religions can make you feel secure in an insecure world, can improve your life, make you a more moral person, give you a sense of your place in the universe, etc. but I'm talking about whether they are True, not whether they are useful. The entire crux of Christianity, as I've said before and will say again until the cows come home (or until Jesus comes back ;)), is the Resurrection. Christianity stands or falls with this. You cannot get rid of the actual, physical, space-time resurrection of Jesus from the dead without eviscerating the very soul of Christianity and reducing it to mere non-threatening life-principles, etc. That's why people have been trying to disprove it for 2000 years!

For the Christian, there is a valid <u>reason</u> to claim to know The Truth, and that is the fact that the Resurrection is the most historically verifiable event in all of ancient history! Thousands of people have taken their axes to the monument of the Resurrection only to have them dulled in defeat. Many of these same people became believers after trying and failing to disprove it! A lawyer named Frank Morison set out to write a book disproving the Resurrection, ended up a believer and wrote a different book instead called *Who Moved the Stone?*, a Christian classic. His first chapter is entitled "The Book That Refused to be Written".

WHO'S GOT GOD?

Yes, Christianity is exclusive in the sense that it claims to be true. The very essence of truth is exclusive. To claim something is true is to claim that something contradictory to it is not true. Your claims about what you believe to be true by necessity exclude contradictory claims. Even the claims that all religions are basically true and that all roads lead to God are exclusivist—they exclude the claim that one religion is *the* truth. So the task becomes, which claims do I choose, and why?

Another interesting thing to think about is the fact that Christianity is the only religion (I think you know I hate that term but I use it to facilitate conversation—try not to attach the usual baggage to the word when I use it) in the world that has significant numbers of believers from every culture. You don't see Nigerian Buddhists, Japanese Jews, Russian Muslims, at least not in any significant numbers. But you do with Christianity. The reason for this, as I said way back when, is that Jesus transcends culture—BECAUSE HE IS TRUE.

Another quote from you:

> *Each religion says God loves us and only us cuz we have the answer.*

Not Christianity. If I haven't convinced you of that by now, then I'm either doing a woeful job over here on my end or you're not listening to what I've been saying. Christianity does say we have the answer, but not that God loves only Christians. How silly.

Another one:

> *So, this is how we have it constructed under the last two thousand years of religion: If God is to grant you your reward in heaven, God expects you to do things his way.*

Well, regardless of whether this is true or not, if God is God, isn't it His right to say that? If you create the game, isn't it your right to make up the rules?

I'm gonna blow your mind again, I hope. In addition to love, did you know that God experiences hatred? I know what you're thinking...but I bet that you believe this too. Don't you believe that God hates murder, hates rape, hates torture with every fiber of His being? Of course He does! But God, being perfect, is able to perfectly hate. It grows organically from the very nature of His love! He doesn't hate like we do, with bitterness, rage and vengeance mixed in—He hates perfectly, just as He loves perfectly.

I'll end with something you said, because I thought it was just awesome:

> *To increase our ability to receive God's abundant love, we must raise our awareness of how big and infinite God is, so that we don't project limits on God's love, for we can only receive God's love in the way that we give our love to God.*

Right on! Your thoughts on the love of God are very passionate and sorely needed in our world today. They are also, if I may use the word, very Christian.

Jeremy

P.S. Tell me about your walk with Jesus—I'm exceedingly curious!

Sent: Thursday, December 7, 2000
Subject: hey!

Jeres,

Don't know why I called you that, just felt moved to. We are in so much agreement. You are so beautiful. I am so honored to know you. I feel the deepest gratitude.

> *Deep in the Consciousness of every Living Human is a cellular memory, we are a race of beings so bright, so glowing in our understandings, so total in our acceptance of Love as the Only Reality, that there is no envy, no anger, no fear, no struggle, judgment, jealousy and no war. We're just people, living together, with love as our only bond, as the only thing we need and want and the only thing we share.*

> *There is no other mandate, no other law, no other dogma, religion, rule, limitation, or instruction. None other is needed.*

> *We live by simple rules: Love is all there is; Do harm to no one; We are all one. Let's suggest a three word code of ethics: Awareness, Honesty, and Responsibility.* [15]

You are so intelligent. Keep going my man. Keep Expanding, and Keep Deepening. Stay in your heart Brother. God is going to increase himself to you. I know it for a fact. You are about to see more God than you ever have before. Don't be tempted to travel up to that well tuned, well running machine between your ears. I know it runs very well, and it's great for certain things, but in this endeavor it will lead you astray.

You and I are God in action.

I couldn't thank you from a deeper place!!!!!

༺༻

From: Jeremy Seely <jeremy_seely@_____.com>
To: Jordan Adams <jadams@_____.net>
Sent: Monday, January 8, 2001
Subject: hey there

Hey Jordan!

How were your holidays? Hopefully they were blessed. Mine were actually pretty stressful, not restful at all. I just had too many places to go and people to see. This year I resolve to make the holidays simpler. Monica and I had some nice time together, though, which was very nice (Ack! I just used 'nice' twice in one sentence!!! My English professor would have me stretched on the rack!).

Well, now that life is somewhat back to normal I can pick up our correspondence. If you remember, you sent me one email in which you asked me several questions that had occurred to you. I believe that I've answered many of them already in our correspondence, but I'll take this opportunity to talk briefly about some of the ones I may not have directly addressed. So here we go…

1. DO YOU BELIEVE WE ARE SEPARATE FROM GOD?

Yes I do. I believe we are created beings, created by this Infinite Being that we call God. God is the Artist, and we are His paintings. He is the Sculptor and we are His pottery. He is the True, Perfect Light, and we are like mirrors, reflecting this light (hopefully). In fact, I look at if we are all mirrors placed at a 45° angle. Above us is the Light—God, and level with us are all the other people we come into contact with throughout our life. In this way we can reflect God's light to others, and through prayer we can reflect others' images back to God by praying for them, etc.

Of course this is an imperfect analogy, as all are, (i.e., God is not just 'above' us, but is all around) but it is a helpful illustration of one aspect of our relationship with God.

2. DO YOU BLIEVE A CHILD OR NEWBORN IS FUNDAMENTALLY WRONG OR SINNED UNTIL HE OR SHE PERFORMS SOMETHING A CERTAIN WAY?

Wow. Here's an emotion-laden question. Let me try to answer it as best I can, because it is a bit complex. I guess the best way is to take a two-pronged approach. First, the Bible states unequivocally that ALL people are born into a condition known as sin. We are, by our very nature, sinful beings—i.e., we like to do things our way. We do what we shouldn't, we don't do what we should, and we do wrong both willfully and ignorantly. David says, *"Surely I was sinful at birth, sinful from the time my mother conceived me"* (Psalms 51:5). That doesn't mean that he was actively doing wrong things inside the womb of his mother, but that, since he was human, the condition of sin existed as part of his very nature starting from the first moment of his conception. Put another way—you're not a sinner because you sin, you sin because you're a sinner. And by the way, I've had several friends tell me that they never were too sure about the idea of original sin until they had babies themselves!

I have a pretty strong feeling, judging from the fact that you have a Catholic background, that behind this question lies another one: do I believe that babies who die before being baptized go to hell? So here's the second prong. There is much debate in Christianity over a term known as the 'age of accountability'. This idea says that people are not held accountable for their sinfulness until they reach an age where they are able to comprehend what sin is and what it means. The reason there is much debate is that this idea is not explicitly taught anywhere in the Bible, but there do seem to be some passages which could support this view. In the end, I must answer that, yes, I do believe all people are fundamentally flawed (we are not 'being all that we can be', or to use your words, our 'cellular memory' tells us that our life now is not as it should be) from conception. As for what happens to babies and children who die very young, I have to honestly respond with "I don't know." But I fully trust that God does the right thing with their souls.

3. DO YOU BELIEVE IN CONDITIONALITY?

I must confess here that I have no idea what you mean. If you mean do I believe that God's love is conditional, I'll answer that later because you asked it a couple questions down. But if you mean something else, can you be more specific?

4. DO YOU BELIEVE HEAVEN IS SOMEWHERE ELSE?

Honestly, I don't really care if it's somewhere else or not. I don't think that's an important question. The Bible does say that eventually order will be restored in this physical universe and we will live here as physical beings, except perfect and undying. We are as caterpillars now, kinda ugly and slow-moving, but when we die we go into our 'cocoon' so to speak and will come out the other side as unbelievably beautiful butterflies. And just as the caterpillar has no idea what is in store for it, so we cannot comprehend just how awesome this new life will be. We simply cannot fathom it. *"No eye has seen, no ear has heard, no mind has conceived what God has prepared for those who love him…"* But unlike the caterpillar, we aren't in complete ignorance of what awaits us, because *"God has revealed it to us by his Spirit"* (1 Cor 2:9-10).

5. DO YOU BELIEVE THAT THERE IS A HELL?

I think I've pretty much answered this one, but yes I do believe in hell. Let me stress again, though, that the biblical definition of hell is a far cry from the caricature of it that you have in your mind. Hopefully I've started to dispel that notion of yours, because it really, truly has no place in an informed person's consciousness.

6. DO YOU BELIEVE THAT GOD JUDGES?

Yes. Perfectly. With the absolute perfect balance of justice, truth, knowledge, mercy, fairness, and love.

7. DO YOU BELIEVE THAT GOD'S LOVE IS CONDITIONAL?

I've answered this many times before, but here it is again…
Of course not!

8. DO YOU BELIEVE THAT YOU NEED ANYTHING?

Are you kidding me? Grace, baby, grace! Without the grace of God I have no idea how horrible my life would be right now, and I don't even want to think about it.

9. DO YOU BELIEVE THAT YOU CREATE YOUR OWN REALITY?

Depends on what you mean. In one sense, no, absolutely not. Reality simply is. In fact, that's the very definition of reality—what is. Reality is reality, no matter what I feel or think about it. If you mean the 'motivational speaker' kind of creating reality, then to a certain extent yes. Our attitudes play a huge role in the things that happen to us, circumstances we find ourselves in, and how we deal with life. To a certain extent, our goals, ambitions, and character-defects (sin) determine much of what happens to us in life. So whatever reality of life we find ourselves in, we generally have had a part in making it so. For example, I don't have a lot of money. Part of that reality is the fact that I wasn't born into wealth, power and prestige. That's something I had no control over. But I have chosen to pursue a career in which there is not a lot of money involved unless you are extremely fortunate. I could have become a lawyer or a doctor, but I chose acting, so I have had a hand in creating the reality I find myself in today.

10. DO YOU BELIEVE THERE IS SUCH A THING AS PUNISHMENT?

Of course I do. That's simply self-evident. Punishment exists. If you mean do I believe there *ought* to be punishment, I still answer yes, but not in a hard, uncaring way. Punishment, when it is given, should always flow out of love, with the desired result of the restoration of the punished individual.

There ya have it. Hope that helps! Once again, these are not answers that I just came up with that sound right to me. I get them from the Bible. It may be that in some cases I am misrepresenting what the Bible has to say. It's very possible, as I am not perfect, all-knowing and all-understanding. So if this is the case, forgive me. The fault is all mine. Talk to you later!

Jeremy

Sent: Monday, January 8, 2001
Subject: Re: hey!

You're right, we are in much agreement. I think we use different language to talk about the same thing in many instances. I'm totally with you on the awareness, honesty and responsibility thing. If only everyone in the world could do their best to live by that…ahhh, it'd be great.

We do still have some critical differences, though, and here's one of 'em. Let me quote you:

> *Don't be tempted to travel up to that well tuned, well running machine between your ears. I know it runs very well, and it's great for certain things, but in this endeavor it will lead you astray.*

Shame on you, Jordan! Don't use your brain?!? Why on earth would God give us a brain if He didn't want us to use it? If I said that to you in encouraging you to place your faith in Jesus (i.e., don't think about it, just belieeeeeeeve), you would see it clearly for what it is. Total propaganda! Eastern, New Age, New Thought—whatever you want to call it—propaganda. What an easy way to get people to blindly follow and ignorantly obey you! Tell them that whenever their mind tells them something isn't quite right with what they're being taught to shut it off because it leads you astray! I know that you of all people are much too smart to fall for something that foolish. I actually used a few of your own words to prove that. Let me quote you from very early on in our writings:

> *I don't believe any book is an infallible guide to be **blindly followed** and **ignorantly obeyed**....if we didn't have to think for ourselves our minds would atrophy.*

You're on shaky ground here, buddy. =) First you're saying we need to use our minds or they'll rot, now you're telling me not to…

Not only that, but it's the perfect copout. Whenever someone presents you with a challenge to your belief-system that may make some sense to you, you can conveniently wave it aside with a quick, "Oh, there's that pesky brain of mine getting in the way again." It's another variant of "don't bother me with the truth, I've already made up my mind" (no pun intended). Stuff like this happens often with teachers of Eastern spirituality. They start off denouncing one facet of "Western" thinking, then ask you to embrace it when referring to their own teachings. As an example, I remember reading a book by Bagwhan Shree Rajneesh (the great OSHO) 2 or 3 years ago. He spends a half-page denouncing faith (this is in the context of a much larger diatribe against Christianity), telling his disciples not to value faith. Then as you skim ahead maybe 4 or 5 pages you see him telling his disciples, "Do not question your spiritual masters. Believe what they tell you without questioning." (paraphrase) Well gee, isn't that the very definition of blind faith?

And last but not least, it is logically, intellectually, practically, and literally impossible not to use your mind, even in matters of the spirit. For you must use your mind to make the determination that you should not use the mind. It is a self-defeating proposition.

I don't want to downplay your emphasis on the heart in this letter, though, Jordan. For what use is a great mind without a great heart? We've seen in history what can happen when that is the case. Conversely, though, what use is a great heart if you have a flabby mind? The one is cold, superior and unmerciful, the other is wishy-washy, easily led, and intellectually dishonest. That's what makes Christianity so great. It is the perfect marriage of the head and the heart. Jesus implores us to have hard heads but soft hearts: *"Be as shrewd as snakes and as innocent as doves,"* and *"Love the Lord your God with all your heart and with all your soul and with all your mind...and love your neighbor as yourself. All the Law and the Prophets hang on these two commandments"* (Matt 10:16, 22:37-40). You see, Christianity can satisfy the mind because it is true, and it can satisfy the heart because we learn through it that God is Love.

I know that you haven't even considered that Christianity might be true for perhaps a long time, but let me urge you once again to do so. Your reasons for rejecting the Catholicism of your childhood are good and reasonable. But I think you're holding on to the stereotypes that you experienced as a kid, which are only reinforced by all the unfair generalizations and ignorant prejudice shown towards Christianity today. To believe in Jesus does not mean becoming a right-winger or a Republican. Jesus had very little to do with politics in His day. He sought to save people, not change laws. And just because there are some very loud-mouthed people out there spewing hatred, bigotry and intolerance in the name of Christ does not mean that's what Christianity is. I sure hope you've gotten at least that much from our months of emails. To be truly open-minded means to be willing to consider anything, not to throw anything out before examining it in an honest manner, to be willing to change your mind, and to walk down whatever path the evidence leads.

Shalom.

-J

Sent: Saturday, January 13, 2001
Subject: Marathon

Jeres,

Hey Buddy! Sorry to hear your holidays were stressful. Funny you mentioned the resolution to simplify your holidays. Last year I made the same

WHO'S GOT GOD?

resolution and it did make all the difference in the world this year. I went to Rhode Island and had a wonderful, slow, peaceful time with the fam in my Mum's new house on the water! God is so very, very generous with me and mine, I am humbled at how lucky I am and the beauty of life!

Thank you very much for directly answering all of my questions. Thank you for having the honesty and skill to do so as well.
I'm afraid we part ways and might not be as close on some issues as I initially thought. In my mind that's ok though, it only proves the many, many different hues or spectrums in the way God "lands" for people. In my opinion, it only highlights the need, nay...dire crucial necessity to remain open to the many ways God can and will communicate with you at the moment.

One such way, as an example, is when I didn't make you wrong for what I determined (in my subjective reality) were "blind spots" on your part. I know you probably feel I have "blind spots" as well :) Well, anyway, when I immediately prayed, "God why can't he see this!!!" God told me maybe you do! Maybe just in another way! Don't judge! It gave me immediate God/Relief, thank God............So with that I'll tell you how God lands for me and we do have substantial difference here.

1. DO YOU BELIEVE WE ARE SEPARATE FROM GOD?

I could give you 30 pages on this one, but a couple of sentences should do: We are not separate from God. How could we be? God is all there is.

2. DO YOU BLIEVE A CHILD OR NEWBORN IS FUNDAMENTALLY WRONG OR SINNED UNTIL HE OR SHE PERFORMS SOMETHING A CERTAIN WAY?

Thank you for the clarification on age of accountability. I must be honest, the whole thing, this arguing over what age a child is guilty, wrong, evil, or sinful is silly, if not sad and dangerous. Love is all there is. Pray on it........

3. DO YOU BELIEVE HEAVEN IS SOMEWHERE ELSE?

> *Honestly, I don't really care if it's somewhere else or not. I don't think that's an important question. The Bible does say that eventually order will be restored in this physical universe and we will live here as physical beings, except perfect and undying. We are as caterpillars now, kinda ugly and slow-moving, but when we die we go into our 'cocoon' so to speak and will come out the other side as unbelievably beautiful butterflies. And just as the caterpillar has no idea what is in store for it, so we cannot comprehend just how awesome this new life will be. We simply cannot fathom it. "No eye has seen, no ear has heard, no mind*

has conceived what God has prepared for those who love him..." But unlike the caterpillar, we aren't in complete ignorance of what awaits us, because "God has revealed it to us by his Spirit.".

I think we're on the same page here. Heaven or Hell can definitely exist right here on earth depending on whether we continually evolve spiritually and follow the examples of the great masters who have revealed who we really are.

4. DO YOU BELIEVE THAT GOD'S LOVE IS CONDITIONAL?

I've answered this many times before, but here it is again...
Of course not!

I don't understand this. Throughout our conversations you have argued for a condition, for a judgment. You have argued for conditions to be met for life in heaven or life in eternal condemnation. You have argued for a God who is saying you must do "x" in a certain way for me to give you "y". This is a condition.

You have argued then for a God who isn't sure whether his children are perfect. For a God who is worried. For a God who isn't quite sure how lovable he is and therefore must make a really, really bad place to punish and hurt his children if they don't choose him.

This to me is not a perfect God, nor the perfect parent. To me, God's love is bigger and better than that. God's love is infinite, bigger than we can possibly ever, ever, ever imagine. Therefore way, way, way bigger than this stupid little intellectual construct we have created of a jealous, angry, limited God. Let it go Jeremy, it's an old, tired construct that doesn't serve you, me, or God anymore.

5. DO YOU BELIEVE THAT YOU NEED ANYTHING?

Are you kidding me? Grace, baby, grace! Without the grace of God I have no idea how horrible my life would be right now, and I don't even want to think about it.

Good! You know you got it!

Shame on you, Jordan! Don't use your brain?!? Why on earth would God give us a brain if He didn't want us to use it?

eh, eh, eh LOL! Sorry, I don't accept shame anymore. That's the old way. I find it squelches the God within. :)

I said "In this instance" your brain doesn't serve you. Please refer to the instance I was talking about in the earlier letter.
Your brain is obviously wonderful, and in very good working order. The instance I was referring to it not serving you is when you continually argue from your "local", subjective reality.

You have argued from one perspective throughout our dialogue.
It is absolutely **Crucial** that you understand this concept if you care at all to understand how God "lands" for me and hundreds of millions of other souls. You, and many others have created a construct. Now that you have created this as the ultimate truth and reality, you must always argue from this point of view. Anything that contradicts this point of view, therefore, especially to the degree to which you're invested in it, is **fearful** and **dangerous** to you to that direct degree. Many people have destroyed others to try not to look at something another way.

Anyway, Buddy, when I look at the body of work we've created, I've gotta laugh. In so many ways our views are polar opposites. In so many blessed ways we say the exact same thing with different languaging.

In Every Way, I deeply value the dialogue because we're in communion with the Divine. We're in communion with each other, and that is just awesome.

೫ೡ

Sent: Sunday, May 27, 2001
Subject: Prayer in Hospitals

Dearest Brother Jeres,

How are you old boy? Long time no chat.

Wanted to share a bit of info I heard last night. Dr. Larry Dossey, a brilliant MD, has been working feverishly to share his medical discoveries of the benefit of prayer for sick people. Over the years his double-blind, peer-reviewed studies have determined beyond a shadow of a doubt that prayer physically positively affects the recovery of his patients. These studies have been replicated time and time again all confirming substantial benefits to the patient when prayer is applied. GOOD NEWS!!

Bad News: When initially enthusiastic Fundamentalist Christians heard that the results showed no difference whether the prayers were Muslim, Jew, Hindu or Christian, they began to slander his work. This to me, is arrogance and ignorance of the highest order. They would rather destroy his work—

and thus hurt or impair the recovery of thousands of sick people—than expand their paradigm and admit that God might be bigger than they initially thought.
I have always agreed with you that God's love is way bigger than we can possibly imagine. That is the reason I refuse to slander her by saying she is so unsure of her lovability that she would burn us (literally) if we don't do it her way. I refuse to slander him by saying he wouldn't heal us if we don't talk to him in a certain language. She's too big for that small, jealous paradigm.

Will you join me in prayer that we all expand our thoughts about who God is? Will you join me in prayer that these "Fundys" stop hurting Dr. Dossey's work? In 1988 only 2 Medical schools allowed the teaching of open prayer for their patients. Now, over 40 do!
The word is out. Even *Science* is starting to begrudgingly admit God's power! Please help me pray for those who limit God's work.

I love you Bro
Jordan

☼☾☽

Sent: Monday, May 28, 2001
Subject: Re: Prayer in Hospitals

Hey Jordan!

Good to hear from you again! We missed you at Monica's party, but I know you were shooting that day. Hopefully it went well! We're planning a trip up to Portland in a couple weeks to check things out up there. My uncle lives up in the Bay area and he's going to show us around—sounds great!

Thank you for sending me that email. I do have to say that I would be extremely skeptical of the source. I imagine you heard that info from a New Thought-type source, did you not? Definitely not unbiased I would say. I highly doubt that "initially enthusiastic" Christians went on to slander this man's work. I say that because I keep myself fairly well-informed about news in the Christian world, and I've never once even *heard* of Dr. Larry Dossey, brilliant MD, much less slanderous attacks on his work. I *have* heard of the many studies that have been, and continue to be, done on the effects of prayer on sick people. What I've gathered leads me to believe that the scientific jury is still out on this one. Some studies have showed positive results, while others have showed no results, and even negative results (i.e., people getting worse, even dying). My own feeling is that this is a ridiculous waste of time in trying to "prove" God. His ways are so far above ours that there is no way we can understand the mysteries of prayer (which I absolutely do believe is heard and cared about by Him). Do we really think that God is merely a genie, and if we rub His bottle by praying He'll do anything we ask Him, i.e., heal all sick people? Of course not. God, and Life, is far too complex for that, and is complicated further by human free will and sin.

Fundamental Christians really are not nearly as evil as New Age/New Thought people would have you believe, Jordan. It's just like politics—Democrats accuse Republicans of being rich, hateful fatcats, and Republicans accuse Democrats of being immoral big-government socialists. Of course, neither is true. It's just propaganda. To be honest, I see more tolerance on the side of conservatives (Christian and otherwise) than the liberals. Liberals, in large measure, are "tolerant" only of people who agree with them, and try to utterly defame anyone who doesn't share their "open-mindedness", as evidenced by this story of supposed Dossey-slandering. I'll grant that perhaps there were a few people or groups that may have done this, but to ascribe that to an entire group of people, most of whom have never even heard of the guy, is simply dishonest and irresponsible. Another great example that comes to mind is the whole issue of the California Defense of Marriage initiative of a couple years ago. Don't misunderstand me—conservatives DO believe certain things are morally and politically wrong, but they are still tolerant. Tolerance is having RESPECT for all opinions and peoples, not AGREEMENT. Two people can have an extremely spirited disagreement about politics, etc. and still be tolerant of each other. Being just a step to the right of center myself, I am in a unique position to see the deficiencies of both sides, and this attempt to redefine tolerance as "what the left believes" is one of the biggest ones I see in the left.

I'll be honest with you now, Jordan. Your sayings about being certain that God doesn't only listen to "one language" of prayer, etc. have always carried a certain weight with me. Much of my spiritual journey of the last seven years has been spent trying to reconcile a tension between what my head knows and what my heart sometimes feels. It is plain from creation that God takes delight in diversity, and there is much beauty in the spirituality of other faiths, from organized religions like Islam and Hinduism all the way down to primitive tribal beliefs. How can one possibly believe that God simply ignores across-the-board every prayer that doesn't end with "in Jesus' name"? On the other hand, the cold, hard historical facts prove nearly incontrovertibly that Jesus really is the one Way, the one Truth, and the one Life. What is one to make of this?

I'll tell you what I've done. For starters, this tension is what has kept me open to learning about and seeing the truth in other spiritual beliefs. It has kept me from identifying with what you would call the "Fundamentalist Christians," or what I would call Christianity—The Religion. I don't believe that true Christianity, i.e., what Jesus came here for, has anything to do with "religion" at all, at least in the connotative sense. Jesus couldn't have been more clear about this, and it's to Christian leaders' discredit that this is exactly what most of the outside world thinks of when they hear the word 'Christianity'. Technically, of course, true Christianity is a religion, in that it is a set of beliefs about, and worship of, God. But most people hear "religion" and <u>think</u> "institutionalized, ritualized sets of do's and don'ts" and "God doesn't like you unless you do it THIS way." As I've said before, that couldn't be farther from the truth about Jesus' mission. Just skim rapidly through even one of the Gospels and this is clear as the noonday sun.

This tension has also caused me to bury my head in the sand at times and not think about or deal with God. It's sent me to that most miserable of places, right in the middle between belief and doubt. As the years pass and I grow more mature, though, I'm becoming more comfortable with this seeming paradox. Life is so complex, and sometimes what is true does seem paradoxical from our point of view—often because we simply don't posses enough understanding. Reality, except for mathematics and maybe a few other things, is not neatly packaged and labeled. I've also learned that the truth is usually somewhere in the middle (kind of like Hegel's Dialectic). This leads me to the certainty that Jesus is the one and only Son of God, but that God also deals with and hears, in His love and justice, people of other faiths in some way. I am certain that, to those who honestly and earnestly seek Him, He will reveal Himself.

It is also helpful to remember that the heart has a dual nature. Yes, it gives us compassion, love and mercy, but it is deceitful and hopelessly sinful, as well. Yes, it clues us into truths that the mind can't grasp, but it also clouds truths that are plain as day. You can't just blindly trust everything your heart is telling you (even though Hollywood says that's the ONLY thing you should trust) without using your mind and looking outside yourself to see if what you feel is true and good. I do my best to look to my heart as well as my mind in figuring out what's right, and it's done me pretty darn well in my life, I must say.

Yes, I will join with you in prayer that <u>all</u> people open their hearts and minds to truths about God that challenge them, because only through challenges can we grow in understanding!

Blessings,

Jeremy

Sent: Monday, May 28, 2001
Subject: Re: Prayer in Hospitals

Bro Jeres,

Well as always you have impressed me and reminded me to get down off my soap box.
You are a remarkable, beautiful man Jeremy. Sure you don't want to come over to the other side? We could use you. :-)

The catch up stuff first: You will love Portland. Be careful, if you go, you won't want to come back. As far as I'm concerned, the only reason to stay in smell-a is if you're doing daily series work. If not, why would anyone live there on purpose? You might as well breathe clean air—Portland has plenty. That show sounds great! Go for it! I've been real fortunate to have the infomercial thing. Thank God it has kept me alive for the last 15 years! If you can get a talk show going or develop a name in game shows or infomercials, it's a wonderfully creative way to make a living. It also gives you the flexibility to live anywhere.

Your deep, heartfelt love for God really comes through in your letter, hence my humble descent off my box.
It reminds me to get back to not judging how other people speak to God. The very thing I accuse "Fundys" of doing, I do right back. This is a great awareness for me, thank you.

The source of the accusation is Dr. Larry Dossey himself. If you go to wisdommedia.com and find the schedule of his TV show you can listen for yourself. This is a real case Jeremy because left wing and moderate Christians love Dr. Dossey. He has been instrumental (understatement) in getting prayer in hospitals, medical schools, and overall acceptance. You said the evidence isn't there for prayer working all the time? The evidence is in, it's double-blind, peer-reviewed, incontrovertible, God works! Even the Hospitals, Doctors, and Medical Schools (i.e., science, former arch-foe of God) are officially changing their stance and begrudgingly admitting the data. Dr. Dossey is being attacked from the right because the data consistently shows no favoritism of one religion over the other. God does not speak the language of religion!

> *Fundamental Christians really are not nearly as evil as New Age/New Thought people would have you believe, Jordan. It's just like politics— Democrats accuse Republicans of being rich, hateful fatcats, and Republicans accuse Democrats of being immoral big-government fascists. Of course, neither is true. It's just propaganda.*

You make a good point here. This to me, highlights one of the pivotal considerations one must always contemplate when dealing with people who think and feel differently about issues. How do we get past our differences? How do we dialogue when both parties feel just as feverishly about their righteousness? How do we do this without accusation?

> *To be honest, I see more tolerance on the side of conservatives (Christian and otherwise) than the liberals. Liberals, in large measure, are "tolerant" only of people who agree with them, and try to utterly defame anyone who doesn't share their "open-mindedness", as evidenced by this story of supposed Dossey-slandering.*

I would venture a guess that many people feel a Liberal is far more tolerant than a Fundy. If a Liberal or a Gay person tried to impose his or her lifestyle on a Right Wing Christian Fundamentalist both legislatively, morally, spiritually, and physically, how tolerant would that Christian be? This is exactly what the game plan is for that Gay person, ask Dr. Falwell or Pat Robertson what they're driving for. That intolerance you see or hear coming from West Hollywood is terror. It's the same kicking, clawing, scratching, and desperation the "Fundy" would be exhibiting if he or she was threatened, if the shoe were on the other foot. I just don't see Dr. Falwell or Pat Robertson as tolerant kindsa guys. I see them as the scariest kinda repressed homophobe (ones with power).
Why do they have so much energy about it? I mean how many times do you think about Gay guys Jeremy? I don't and I'm sure you don't give it a second thought. I don't care!! That fat sh*t Falwell s attracted to Rob Lowe and it's a part about himself that he hates and can't come to terms with, so he'll destroy it. :-) just a theory, (it might be Robertson who wants his ass)

> *there is much beauty in the spirituality of other faiths, from organized religions like Islam and Hinduism all the way down to primitive tribal beliefs.*

"*All the way down*" to primitive tribal beliefs? Do you hear the inherent judgment and value statement about the *level* or quality or accuracy of another's way of speaking to God? You've given it a rating. We all have these blind spots and judgments, and prejudices. Many people feel "primitive" tribal beliefs are way *closer* to God because they Live God.
A lot of Native beliefs are deep rooted in the *experience* of God. They be-

lieve as soon as you start labeling, characterizing, proselytizing, claiming and monopolizing God you have lost God. As soon as you put your little human judgment on God you missed it, you didn't get it, you don't know God. Calling their way of communicating with God wrong only shows how much we don't get God. It shows how little we think God is. God is way bigger than our "conversation" about who God is. I know you know what I mean about conversation. Not our little one right here, but mankind's...

The degree to which we keep trying to fit God into our little paradigm is the direct degree to which we'll keep hurting each other over our little concepts. Not what God wants.
Peace Brother
I love you.
-Jordan

ಙಚಃ

Sent: Tuesday, May 29, 2001
Subject: Re: Prayer in Hospitals

Hey Jordan,

That was an outstanding response to my letter, bro. Are you sure YOU don't want to come over to OUR side? We could use you over here, too, heh heh.

I went over to wisdommedia and looked around. Pretty cool website. I found some stuff on Dr. Dossey but I didn't have the inclination to listen to every guest appearance he's ever had there in order to hear his claim about the Christians slandering his work. In any event, I said already that I don't doubt that there may have been a few people or groups who have publicly criticized him, but in no way do they speak for all of Christianity—as if any one person could, anyway!

> *How do we get past our differences? How do we dialogue when both parties feel just as feverishly about their righteousness? How do we do this without accusation?*

Extraordinarily perceptive and sensitive! How DO we do this? SHOULD we do this? SHOULD all views be treated as equal, and just live as let live, or should we debate them vigorously yet civilly in order to reach a further understanding? I think the best way to go about this is to use Jesus' model. He basically said, "Here's the truth. If you're interested, come follow me and learn more. If not, well it's your loss, but I still love you." The only people He forced His truths on were the hypocritical religious people who, in His words, *"tie up heavy loads and put them on men's shoulders, but themselves are not willing to lift a finger to move them,"* who *"travel over land and sea to win a single convert, and when he becomes one, you make him twice as much a son of hell as you are,"* and *"are like whitewashed tombs, which look beautiful on the outside but on the inside are full of dead men's bones and everything unclean. In the same way, on the outside you appear to people as righteous but on the inside you are full of hypocrisy and wickedness!"* Matt. 23:4-28

> *If a Liberal or a Gay person tried to impose his or her lifestyle on a Right Wing Christian Fundamentalist both legislatively, morally, spiritually, and physically, how tolerant would that Christian be?*

But that is exactly what the gay agenda is, Jordan. They're not after basic civil rights - our Constitution and Declaration of Independence already gives them that. They're after special rights, they're trying to force people who have legitimate moral and spiritual objections to the practice of homosexuality to accept their views as right, good, and healthy. No one on the right wants to take away basic human rights from gay people, but the homosexual community is trying very hard to make it ILLEGAL to object to homosexuality. Conservatives are saying nothing more than, "I think homosexuality is a sin." This was so blatantly obvious during the whole Prop. 22 campaign![16] The gays went on a rampage against people like Knight and anyone else who believes that marriage is, by its very definition, a union between one man and one woman. I read scores of letters in newspapers and magazines during that whole period and the level of intolerance shown by the gay/liberal community was astonishing, especially in contrast to the sensitivity the supporters of the Proposition were showing. I strongly disagree with the notion that this comes from terror. By and large, gay people are not in danger of their lives in this country, and they've done some great work in getting the country to talk about these issues and come to grips with the fact that we can't bury our heads in the sand and pretend they don't exist. But I sense such an arrogance and such a sense of moral superiority over those who disagree with them, Jordan, it really sickens me.

As for Falwell and Robertson, to be honest, I really don't have any idea of the kinds of things they say, since I don't listen to either one of them. For all I know, they could be good guys who get blasted totally unfairly by the left. But if they really are as hateful as people say they are, then that just proves what I said in the last letter about those Christians in public leadership roles who give us all a bad name. They certainly do not represent all Christians, even all conservative Christians, which should be self-evident I hope. Unfortunately, though, in this Jerry

Springer day and age, it's far easier to set up a simple straw-man target and beat it to a bloody pulp than to really sit down and discuss our disagreements.

> *That fat sh*t Falwell is attracted to Rob Lowe and it's a part about himself that he hates and can't come to terms with, so he'll destroy it. :-) just a theory, (it might be Robertson who wants his ass)*

I know you're kidding here, but this is a perfect example of what I'm talking about!

> *there is much beauty in the spirituality of other faiths, from organized religions like Islam and Hinduism all the way down to primitive tribal beliefs.*

Thank you for pointing out my poor choice of words here. What you said in reply is pretty right on, except the description of native beliefs was a little romanticized. They fought religious wars as well. Your main point is accurate, though. Of course, the comparison I was making was in terms of size and organization (i.e., Islam and Hinduism have about a billion followers each and are very well-organized, *all the way down* to primitive tribal beliefs which have at most a few thousand followers each and are much looser in structure). I should have been more precise in my wording so as to prevent the confusion. I would hope that after all this time you would know me well enough to realize I would never say something like that.

Well, there was a little more I wanted to write, but I'm feeling sick and its getting late so I think I'll cut off my long-windedness. =)
Thank you for all the thought-provoking conversations we've had. They're a blessing!

Jeremy

Sent: Wednesday, May 30, 2001
Subject: Re: Prayer in Hospitals

I find myself shaking my head yes to your letter. Agreed! Your letters are a blessing to me too. We are dialoguing and you are informing me, reminding me, and helping me. So glad I know you!
More later.

Blessings,
Jordan

From: Jordan Adams <jadams@_____.net>
To: Jeremy Seely <jeremy_seely@_____.com>
Sent: Wednesday, July 18, 2001
Subject: Party this Sunday

Hello everybody,

I'd like to invite you all to my place for a party this Sunday. Food, fun, and fellowship with friends! Let me know if you can make it!

Jordan

ಇಂಬ

Sent: Thursday, July 19, 2001
Subject: Re: Party this Sunday

J

Thanks for the invite. I won't be able to attend—I'm playing Cassius in a production of *Julius Caesar* and we rehearse on weekends. Have fun!

J

Sent: Saturday,, July 21, 2001
Subject: Re: Party this Sunday

Isn't Cassius the bad guy? Maybe I'm wrong. Anyway, if you study Caesar at all, you'll find him fascinating. He was to some extent one of the first

Jeffersonian Democrats – believing a "congress" and the people not only had the right – but could do a much better job at "making the calls."

I believe he was also "offed" ... What is it with the people who make the "call" getting offed? IE: Jesus, Gandhi, M.L.K., J.F.K., R.F.K., Abraham Lincoln, John Lennon, etc.
It seems the people with the purest, most loving, peaceful message attract the most vile among us who then strike them down.
My theory is when a truth dispenser holds up the mirror and says this is how things could be, you have two choices – you can look at your actions and how you've been and be honest with yourself and correct your actions – or you have to make that messenger wrong. When the messenger has a particularly "loud" voice, and your denial is psychically entrenched, your cognitive dissonance is such that you must quiet that voice, or go mad.

Blessings,
-Jordan

☙☼❧

Sent: Monday, July 23, 2001
Subject: Portland

Dear Jordache (don't know why I felt like calling you that),

As I said earlier, we're back from Portland. It was beautiful! Less people, less stress…fresh-smelling air! It actually felt healthy to breath in a great lung full of air…imagine that. The area was subliminally much more peaceful as well. Unlike here in SoCal, outdoor advertising hardly exists. Your eyes aren't assaulted at every turn in every nook and cranny in existence by billboards, neon signs, and the like. And the thousands of old, wizened trees bear a silent witness to the value of the slow, calm, and reflective way of life. Another great thing about Portland is the perfect balance between big city convenience/stimulation and the close proximity of untouched natural beauty, encouraging spirituality and contemplation of the wonders of God.

Your short musing about how great people always seem to end up getting 'offed' was fascinating, and something I've also thought about. Your theory sounds pretty darn good to me, bro! I'm with you on that train! I'm going to follow this up in a bit with another letter that's kind of back on track with the whole spiritual theme we've been discussing over the past year, as there were a few loose ends I wanted to clarify.

Many blessings to you,

Jeremy

P.S. Oops, I almost forgot! (not really, heh heh heh) Congratulations are in order, as Monica and I became engaged last Saturday while in Portland!!!!!!!!!!!!! We're planning to get married next spring or summer, down here in California. You will, of course, be invited, so keep all your weekends next year free, heh heh! =)

Sent: Tuesday, July 24, 2001
Subject: Re: Portland

Jeres,

If you move to Portland I'll be eternally jealous! Just kidding, I'm excited to get out of the dust bowl myself. I have a couple o' jobs brewing here and once those commitments are fulfilled, I'm outta here!

Congratulations on the engagement! I couldn't think of two more awesome people to be together. Your children are going to be so fortunate to have parents like you! Just think, there's children right now who are "in the mist" waiting to "miracalize" you. One minute "not here" then, in a short time little bundles of joy on the earth! A very strong argument for God's existence is to just observe that. One minute not here - the next – here. Next time an Atheist says "prove God's existence" just say "we're here" and walk away. ;-)

Thanks for the honoring of the invite. I'll be there with bells on....Well maybe not bells, that might be a bit distracting. Maybe a bright tie.

With a happy heart,
-Jordan

ಬಿಚ

Sent: Wednesday, July 25, 2001
Subject: Loose Ends

Dear Jordache,

Thank you so much for your kind words! I hold dear all the joy people have expressed at our engagement. If nothing else in my life went right from now until I die, I would still be eternally grateful to God for sending me someone who fits with me so perfectly. You're so right about the existence of God—creation happening right before our eyes! Well, in a couple years, anyway... =)

Anyway, to our work, alive! --Sorry, just had to slip in a *Julius Caesar* reference in there. Like I said, I wanted to address a few loose ends in our dialogue that, for whatever reason, I never got around to responding to but always wanted to. First let me say that our letters have been instructive to me and highly valued as well as enjoyed. It's interesting how much we have in common even though we have radically different views on some bedrock issues, isn't it? I think the rest of the world could do worse than take note of that.
A while back you wrote something about your view of God:

> *We are not separate from God. How could we be? God is all there is.*

I can agree with you in one sense of this, in the way that a painting is not separate from its painter. But my question to you would be this: if God is literally all there is, and if literally all is God, then what do you make of all the evil in the world? Is God the rapist? Is God the murderer? Is God the conquistador? Is God the African who captured and sold a rival tribe-member to a European slave-trader? Is God that slave-trader? Is God the man who bought that slave? IS GOD EVIL? It seems impossible for me to believe that the Divine is everything, and at the same time believe that the Divine is unconditionally loving and all-good. God must be really confused if He/She/It is both the murderer and the judge who condemns the murderer. The Christian view of God makes infinitely more sense.

There was also a point at which you advised me not to use my brain in a certain instance and I retorted back by saying what good's a brain if we're not meant to use it. Thank you for standing up for what you said and pointing out that your comment was not meant to be applied across the board, but only in the particular situation you were talking about. I humbly apologize for exaggerating your statement and taking your words out of context. I can't stand it when I see others do that, and I am vexed (I am terribly vexed) to see that I myself have done the very same thing. Embarrassing. Just goes to show that none of us are perfect, eh? ;)
I still, however, disagree with your intended point, heh heh. As I've said before, I think it absolutely essential to use both the heart and the mind in all areas of life, even and especially when talking about spiritual truths. You explained to me how I argue from one perspective, one view, throughout our dialogue—I mostly agree. You go on to say:

> *Now that you have created this as the ultimate truth and reality, you must*

> *always argue from this point of view. Anything that contradicts this point of view, therefore, esp. to the degree to which you're invested in it, is **fearful** and **dangerous** to you to that direct degree.*

First of all, I feel I should point out that you too have done this. Everyone has, no one can escape it. Your 'construct' is much, much different than mine, but you still have a definite 'construct' of ultimate truth and reality, and you have been arguing from this point of view. Your construct says that all constructs are valid, that there are as many paths to God as there are people, and that no one's view is really wrong. Your construct says (if I have read you correctly) that one should not use logic/mental prowess in the search for, and communion with, God. Your construct says that 'God' is unconditionally loving, that there is no such place as hell, that all is God, etc.

Many people proudly point out that this construct is so open-minded, so progressive, so much more 'inclusive' than their supposedly bigoted and narrow-minded neighbors, but even the broadest of the so-called 'inclusive' beliefs are really exclusive at the core, because they by nature exclude the many beliefs in only one way to God! Not only does this construct exclude those beliefs, it often looks arrogantly down its nose at them, as if they are somehow less evolved, less intelligent. Perhaps you might say, "No it doesn't exclude them, it simply sees the truth in all of them, it sees that they're all true, and if you could just get past the 'I'm right' syndrome, you'd see it too." I don't think people who say things like that realize how offensive that is to a truly spiritual Jew, Christian, Moslem, Hindu, etc. It's like saying, "I'm smarter than you, I'm higher than you, and I can see that your most cherished beliefs don't matter, because basically all religions can be reduced to the lowest common denominator—Be nice to each other." In addition to not being true, this is the very attitude that they most detest in others! "I'm right and you're wrong. Your view of God as Allah/Jesus/Yahweh/Krishna is misguided, or at best only partially true." This way of thinking is also violent in a way, for it annexes other people's religious beliefs without asking their permission, redefines them in the way it wants to, and takes them for its own.

So, everybody believes that their view is right (obviously, else why would they believe it?). This is why it's so important for people to discuss spiritual differences, because they can't all be all right, for there are certain irreconcilable differences embedded in them. Jesus can't be the Son of God and not be the Son of God. God can't be an impersonal 'Force' and a personal Being. Hell cannot both exist and not exist. As Lincoln said, "Both [of us] may be, and one must be, wrong," no matter how un-P.C. that may sound. By discussing them, we can endeavor to discover which beliefs, if any, are worthy of being believed as true, which beliefs have good reason for being believed. The only person with a truly wide-open construct is the absolute agnostic, who says "I don't know <u>anything</u> for sure. For all I know, you could all be right and you could all be wrong." I'm sure that many New-Thought type people arrived at New-Thought for this very reason. "Since we're only human and we can't know anything for absolute certainty, it's better to celebrate the samenesses we all have and let everyone worship as they see fit, doing violence to none." This is a view that I definitely respect and I see the incredible value in it. Personally, I like to combine these two feelings, "Worship and let worship" with "Let's talk about our differences and try to come up with the truth." If there's an open door to talk about spirituality with someone, I love to do it, as we've been doing. But if the guy ain't interested, he ain't interested!

Now, you say that using my brain doesn't serve me because it prevents me from breaking out of an established 'box' (my view of the universe) and compels me to continually argue from my local and subjective view, is that right? I can see that to be true and be a negative thing if I am using my brain incorrectly, or am only using part of my brain. If I use my brain, though, in a responsible manner, balance it with my heart, examine my will to see if my intentions are honest, and ask God for help, it is a positive thing. If this box my brain has led me to construct is contained in that part of the universe that is Truth, then it is good that I used my brain. And if my box happens to lie in that which is unTruth, then my brain, if it is in good working order and used responsibly, should alert me to that fact and prompt me to move my box elsewhere. I know that we always say "Don't put God in a box," etc. True, true. This way, I'm not putting God in a box, I'm bringing my box <u>to</u> God and plunking it right down in the middle. And if I make sure that I keep the lid open on my box, I am always available for new thoughts and Truth that I may not have known before. If I keep the lid open, I can still hold on to a certain set of beliefs, but I also remain free to allow God to increase Himself to me.

One "yeahbut" that you may throw at me is the idea I touched on above: how can we, in our limitedness and unimaginable ignorance have any idea whatsoever what and where Truth is? I mean, after all, there is an infinite amount of stuff to know about The Universe. All of humanity put together knows perhaps the smallest, most microscopic speck of this knowledge. Who are we then to claim to know God and to know what the Truth is? I don't know about you but for me that has long been a stumbling block to placing my faith in a certain way of looking at God. This train of thought kept me from God for a long while…until I realized that I was stopping the train too soon. Yes, we know only the smallest particle of knowledge, but God is infinite and knows all (I love the phrase 'but God'. It's one of the most hopeful phrases there are!). He knows exactly where that one speck of knowledge is and He has the power to descend right down into that speck and enlighten us about the rest. Of course we'll never <u>comprehend</u> it all, but with God's help we can certainly <u>apprehend</u> it. The question then becomes, has God done this, and in what way? Obviously you know my answers to those questions, and I believe I have rock-solid reasons to continue to hold on to those answers. I still keep myself ever open, though, because I know I don't know it all. Remaining open also has the side-benefit of preventing arrogance in one's beliefs. There are only two beliefs about God that I hold which are not up for revision at any time: 1) A personal God (trans-personal, if you want to be technical) exists who Loves me, and 2) Jesus was His incarnation, died and rose from the dead. The reason they're not up for revision is not because I've closed my mind on the matter, but because the amount of testifying evidence in every single area of my life, every nook and cranny of my very existence—emotional, logical, and experiential—is so incredibly, massively in support of those two beliefs that I can't even imagine anything ever coming along in the future that could shake my faith in them. Beyond that, though, pretty much everything else I believe is always open to revision...if I can be persuaded. =]

Whew. Almost done. A recurring topic in your letters is your difficulty in understanding how Christians can claim God to be unconditionally loving in one breath, and talk about conditions needed for life in heaven in the next. I think I've done a good job of explaining this in all my letters, but maybe the kernel got lost in all my long-windedness. Very basically, God has absolutely no conditions at all for you or anyone else to receive His love. He loves everyone, including the most vile scum of the earth. According to the Bible, though, there is a condition for SALVATION, and that has something to do with Jesus, his death and resurrection. Salvation is different from love, d'ye see? God's Love is unconditional. God's Salvation is not. Before you go into another harangue about a cartoon God who petulantly throws good people into a really, really bad place when they don't talk to him the way he wants them to, though, please reread all that I've written about the subjects of hell, salvation, and free will. In lieu of that, I can't recommend highly enough the chapters on hell and salvation in a book called *The Handbook of Christian Apologetics* by Kreeft and Tacelli. Perhaps, if you read either, you'll finally be persuaded to drop that caricature and tackle the ideas for what they really are. You are absolutely right when you say it's an old, tired construct—it's not the Christians who hold to it, though, but their detractors, either out of ignorance or a deliberate attempt to distort the facts!

One final, short thought. The reason why people in the religious community (not just Christians, but mostly so) speak out so much against homosexuality is not that they're repressed homos themselves, or that they're self-righteous prigs (though some are). It's because there is a large portion of the population that believes homosexuality is perfectly normal and healthy, and speak out just as loudly in defense of it. Same thing with anti-abortion groups. You'd see Christians, Jews, and probably even New-Thought people doing just the same thing if a group came out proclaiming stealing as healthy and moral. It's really as simple as that (not that I'm equating homosexuality with stealing, please don't think that).

Blessings,

Jeremy

Sent: Friday, July 27, 2001
Subject: Re: Loose Ends

Mr. Seely,

As always, I am deepened and warmed by your thoughtful, reflective, profound, intimate missives. Enough adjectives? Sorry, they're just inspired by your work.

I do find it very interesting and awesome that in our persuasions or attempts at persuading each other, we have many times stumbled onto common ground. I find it instructive for me when that happens, it reminds me of how much I don't know, and the dire importance of not judging others. I want to add that I seem to always end up focusing on where we don't agree and that does not paint an accurate picture of our relationship. There are so many times when I think "oh Jeremy would dig this" and also when I read your notes there's tons I agree with and I know I haven't pointed that out enough in the past. One of the things I really like about you is your open-mindedness and quest for knowledge. It is refreshing.

As you and Julius say: To our work alive! You touched on one of the biggies in your first paragraph: If I'm saying God is all there is, how could there be evil? You went in to great detail on the different evils which have occurred on this planet. How could God have been a part of that? Obviously, not an easy question so please pardon the long answer:

Jeremy, we are all perfect already. Yes, even with the mistakes. What

WHO'S GOT GOD?

about the evil?

There is no evil. Huh!?

Listen to this excerpt from *Conversations With God (Book 2)* by Neal Donald Walsch in which God has a conversation with the author:

> **A tree is no less perfect because it is a seedling. A tiny infant is no less perfect than a grown-up. It is perfection itself. Because it cannot *do* a thing, does not *know* a thing, that does not make it somehow less perfect.**
>
> **A child makes mistakes. She stands. She toddles. She falls. She stands again, a bit wobbly, hanging on to her mommy's leg. Does that make the child imperfect?**
>
> **I tell you it is just the opposite! The child is *perfection itself*, wholly and completely adorable.**

But the child hasn't done anything wrong! The child hasn't consciously disobeyed, hurt another, damaged herself.

> **The child doesn't *know* right from wrong.**

Precisely.

> **Neither do you.**

But I *do*. I know that it is wrong to kill people, and it is right to love them. I know that it is wrong to hurt and right to heal them, to make things better. I know that it is wrong to take what is not mine, to use another, be dishonest.

> **I could show you instances where each one of these "wrongs" would be right.**

You're playing with me now.

> **Not at all. Merely being factual.**

If you're saying there are exceptions to every rule, then I agree.

> **If there are *exceptions* to a rule, then it is not a rule.**

Are you telling me that it is *not* wrong to kill, to hurt, to take from another?

That depends on what you are trying to do.

Okay, okay, I get it. But that doesn't make these things *good*. Sometimes one has to do bad things to achieve a good end.

Which doesn't make them "bad things" at all, then, does it? They are just means to an end.
Are you saying the end justifies the means?

What do you think?

No. Absolutely not.

So be it.
Don't you see what you're doing here? You're *making up the rules as you go along*!
And don't you see something else? *That's perfectly okay*.
It's what you're *supposed* to be doing!
All of life is a process of deciding Who You Are, and then experiencing that.
As you keep expanding your vision, you make up new rules to cover that! As you keep enlarging your idea about your Self, you create new do's and don'ts, yeses and nos to encircle that. These are the boundaries that "hold in" something which *cannot* be held in.
You cannot hold in "you," because you are as boundless as the Universe. Yet you can create a *concept* about your boundless self by imagining, and then accepting, *boundaries*.
In a sense, this is the only way you can know yourself as anything in particular.
That which is boundless is boundless. That which is limitless is limitless. It cannot exist anywhere, because it is everywhere. If it is *everywhere*, it is *nowhere in particular*.
God is everywhere. Therefore, God is nowhere in particular, because to be somewhere in particular, God would have to *not be somewhere else*—which is *not possible for God*.
There is only one thing that is "not possible" for God, and that is for God to not be God. God cannot "not be." Nor can God not be like itself. God cannot "un-God" Itself.
I am everywhere, and that's all there is to it. And since I am *everywhere*, *I am nowhere*. And if I am NOWHERE, where am I?
NOW HERE....Do you see how you have created your ideas of "right" and "wrong" simply to *define Who You Are*?
Do you see that without these definitions—boundaries—you are nothing?
And do you see that, like Me, you keep changing the boundaries

as you change your ideas of Who You Are?

Well, I get what You are saying, but it does not seem that I have changed the boundaries—my own personal boundaries—very much. To me it has always been wrong to kill. It has always been wrong to steal. It has always been wrong to hurt another. The largest concepts by which we govern ourselves have been in place since the beginning of time, and most human beings agree on them.

Then why do you have war?

Because there will always be some who break the rules. There's a rotten apple in every barrel.

What I'm going to tell you now, and in the passages which follow, may be very difficult for some people to understand and accept... there are no "rotten apples." There are only people who *disagree with your point of view on things*, people who construct a different model of the world. No persons do anything inappropriate, given their model of the world.

Then their "model" is all messed up. I know what's right and wrong, and because some other people don't, that doesn't make *me* crazy because I *do*. *They're* the ones who are crazy!

I'm sorry to say that's exactly the attitude which starts wars.

I know, I know. I was doing that on purpose. I was just repeating here what I've heard many other people say. But how can I answer people like that? What *could* I say?

You could tell them that people's ideas of "right" and "wrong" change—and have changed—over and over again from culture to culture, time period to time period, religion to religion, place to place...even from family to family and person to person. You could point out to them that what many people considered "right" at one time—burning people at the stake for what was considered witchcraft, as an example—is considered "wrong" today.
You could tell them that a definition of "right" and "wrong" is a definition established not only by time, but also by simple geography. You could allow them to notice that some activities on your planet (prostitution, for instance) are illegal in one place, and, just a few miles down the road, legal in another. [17]

But Jordan what about the absolutes I've told you about in all of my letters to you? Are you even reading my letters!!!!!!

Yes, Jeres, I have :-) I am talking about the absolutes.

Listen to another excerpt from Conversations with God (Book 2): Let's take Hitler, within our paradigm he's pretty easy to see as an absolute. Absolute evil. Just about every religion in the world has declared him condemned and sent straight to hell.

> **Now your thought that Hitler is a monster is based on the fact that he ordered the killing of millions of people, correct?**

Obviously, yes.

> **Yet what if I told you that what you call "death" is the *greatest thing that could happen to anyone*—what then?**

I'd find that hard to accept.

> **You think that life on Earth is better than life in heaven? I tell you this, at the moment of our death you will realize the greatest freedom, the greatest peace, the greatest joy, and the greatest love you have ever known. Shall we therefore punish Bre'r Fox for throwing Bre'r rabbit into the briar patch?**

You are ignoring the fact that, no matter how wonderful life after death may be, our lives here should not be ended against our will....

> **...life is often cut short by many things...a hurricane, an earthquake...**

That's different. You're talking about an act of God.

> ***Every* event is an act of God.**
> **Do you imagine that an event could take place if I did not want it to? Do you think that you could so much as lift your little finger if I chose for you not to? You can do *nothing* if I am against it.**
> **Yet let us continue to explore this idea of "wrongful" death together. Is it "wrong" for a life to be cut short by disease?**

"Wrong" isn't a word that applies here. Those are natural causes. That's not the same as a human being like Hitler murdering people.

> **What about an accident? A stupid accident—?**

Same thing. It's unfortunate, tragic, but that's the Will of God. We can't peer into God's mind and find out why these things happen. We ought not try, because God's Will is immutable and incomprehensible. To seek to unravel Divine Mystery is to lust for knowledge beyond our ken. It is sinful.

How do you know?

Because if God wanted us to understand all of this, we *would*. The fact that we *don't—can't*—is evidence that it is God's *will* that we don't.

I see. The fact that you don't *understand* it is evidence of God's Will. The fact that it *happens* is *not* evidence of God's will. Hmmmm...

I guess I'm not very good at explaining some of this, but I know what I believe.

Do you believe in God's Will, that God is All Powerful?

Yes.

Except where Hitler was concerned. What happened there was *not* God's Will.

No.

How can that be?

Hitler violated the Will of God.

Now how do you think he could do that if My Will is all powerful?

You allowed him to.

If I allowed him to, then it was *My Will* that he should.

It would seem that way...but what possible *reason* could You have? No. It was Your Will that he have Free Choice. It was *his* will that he do what he did.

You're so close on this. So close.
You're right, of course. It was My Will that Hitler—that *all* of you— have Free Choice. But it is *not* My Will that you be punished unceasingly, unendingly, if you do not make the choice I want you to make. If that were the case, how "free" have I made your choice? Are you really free to do what you want if you know you'll be made to suffer

unspeakably if you do not do what I want? What kind of choice is that?

It isn't a question of punishment. It's just Natural Law. It's simply a question of consequences.

> I see you've been schooled well in all the theological constructions that allow you to hold Me as a vengeful God—without making Me responsible for it.
> But who *made* these Natural Laws? And if we can agree that I must have put them into place, why would I put into place such laws—then give you the power to overcome them?
> If I didn't want you affected by them—if it was My Will that My wonderful beings never should suffer—why would I create the possibility that you could?
> And then, why would I continue to tempt you, day and night, to break the laws I've set down?

You don't tempt us. The devil does.

> There you go again, making Me not responsible.
> Don't you see that the only way you can rationalize your theology is to render Me powerless? Do you understand that the only way your constructions make sense is if Mine *don't*?
> Are you really comfortable with the idea of a God who creates a being whose actions it cannot control?

I didn't say You can't control the devil. You can control *everything*. You're *God*! It's just that You *choose not to*. You allow the devil to tempt us, to try to win our souls.

> But why? Why would I do that if I don't want to have you not return to Me?

Because You want us to come to You out of choice, not because there is no choice. You set up Heaven and Hell so there could be a choice. So we could act out of choosing, and not out of simply following a path because there is no other.

> I can see how you've come to this idea. That's how I've set it up in your world, and so you think that's how it must be in *Mine*.
> In your reality, Good cannot exist without Bad. So you believe it must be the same in Mine.
> Yet I tell you this: There is no "bad" where I Am. And there is no Evil. There is only the All of Everything. The Oneness. And the Awareness,

> the Experience, of that.
> Mine is the Realm of the Absolute, where One Thing does not exist in relationship to Another, but quite independent of anything.
> Mine is the place where All There Is is Love. [18]

So, my dear Jeres, this is my long, long, winded way of saying that I believe we continually evolve. Our notion of God and God's power continually deepens. Our understanding of truth, our relationship with the all mighty grows. It is a process. Our notions of God's motivations and reasonings expands as we let go of old concepts of duality.

Above all I say this: God is love. I know for a fact that God is bigger, better, and more loving than the punishment paradigm.

Let me also tip my hat to your for your acknowledgement of:

> *I humbly apologize for exaggerating your statement and taking your words out of context. I can't stand it when I see others do that, and I am vexed (I am terribly*
> *vexed) to see that I myself have done the very same thing. Embarrassing. Just goes to show that none of us are perfect, eh? ;)*

This is such a high value you have displayed here. It is the ability to step out of ourselves and honestly assess and correct.
Wow! You are an inspiration to me. I hope you don't mind if I model you.

I love you Brother. This correspondence is blessing for me.

Stay well.
Jordan

ps
if there's specific things I didn't address in your letter please let me know.

❧

Sent: Friday, July 27, 2001
Subject: Addendum

I realized I didn't address a section of your last letter – which I can't find now! – so I'll go off memory. In one paragraph you were very clear about your non-negotiables and it left me with the impression – false or not – that you thought I was trying to get you to "give them up" or think another way. Let me be clear that the spirituality I most resonate with is adamantly against this. The spirituality I most love would find that most unacceptable

– a spiritual violence. That isn't to say I follow it perfectly. Far from it. I know my ego gets in there and wants the other to see it my way. It is only to say the goal is to not judge another's path. One of my other goals is to watch, observe, learn and enjoy God working his miracles in your life through your chosen conduit. It is so beautiful and awesome to watch her grace wash over you, bless you, and bring you closer to your soul mate. That is where I choose to reside. So, to the degree that I've made you feel your path is wrong I humbly apologize from the deepest place. I *know* you have a relationship with God and it blesses me to know you.

☙☜

Sent: Saturday, July 28, 2001
Subject: Re: Addendum

Hey Jordan,

Thanks for that addendum, it was very touching. I didn't mean to imply that you were trying to annex *my* beliefs or get me to give them up—I think I know you better than that now. =P I know you don't follow your ideals perfectly, and neither do I by a long shot. In fact, just today I had an argument with Monica over something really stupid because neither one of us wanted to let go of our pride in "being right", and in another conversation we had today I realized later that I was not showing any love or mercy toward the type of people we were talking about. No one who is truly concerned with having a relationship with God can follow their ideals perfectly, because we're not perfect (or, as you would say, we ARE perfect but just haven't realized it yet. I come at it from a different angle: we aren't perfect, but we have the *potential* to be.) But it's a good sign when a person realizes how far short they fall of their own ideals, for it is said that the more truly spiritual a person is, the more aware they are of their sin (which literally means "missing the mark"). The apostle Paul, who is one of the small percentage of Christians who can honestly say they gave their whole lives over to Christ, and who was a pinnacle of Christian virtue (and wrote half the New Testament, for goodness' sake), said this:

> *I do not understand what I do. For what I want to do I do not do, but what I hate I do. I have the desire to do what is good, but I cannot carry it out. For what I do is not the good I want to do; no, the evil I do not want to do—this I keep on doing.*
>
> *When I want to do good, evil is right there with me. For in my inner being I delight in God's law; but I see another law at work in the members of my body, waging war against the law of my mind and making me a prisoner of the law of sin at work within my members. What a wretched man I am! Who will rescue me from this body of death?*

This from a man who lived the Christian life about as purely and completely as is possible! He concludes by answering his own question:

Thanks be to God—through Jesus Christ our Lord! Romans 7:15-25

Truer words were never spoken, at least as far as my inner life is concerned. I personally draw much hope and encouragement from this short segment of his letter, because I totally relate to it!

It is clear to me that you also are relating to God and seeking truth. I'm sure that, if we both keep our spirits truly open to God and truth, we'll be seeing a lot of each other in eternity, however it all works out. I want to also respond to the longer letter you wrote me, but it will obviously take more time than this short reply. I'll get it to you in a few days. Blessings to you, bro!

Sent: Saturday, July 28, 2001
Subject: Re: Addendum

Thanks Jeres,

Wow, that passage from Apostle Paul is powerful. I agree, and laugh at myself when I want to jump ahead to spiritual revelation, and just be *there* already. I should be spending so much more time in contemplation, meditation and prayer – and keeping my yapper shut ;-)

Funny thought: God gave us one mouth and *two* ears. We should use them proportionally. That's my goal. So I affirm: Thank you God for giving me Jeremy as a friend and allowing me to witness his love and burning desire for you.

I know we agree that we all need to spend a lot more time in gratitude.

You're awesome Mr. Seely

Love,
-Jordan (El Jordano)

Sent: Monday, August 27, 2001
Subject: Conversations…

Jordan,

I know I said I'd get back to you in a few days. Sorry it's been so long. I know what you're talking about—it seems that we focus so much on our points of divergence (which is true), but that's only because our differences are the interesting things to talk about. It'd be pretty boring if all we did was write "I agree!" and "Right on!" back and forth. But it is definitely true that we see eye to eye on a whole lot of stuff.

You used a lot of stuff from *Conversations With God* in your last letter, so I'd like to talk about that book. I've read a good chunk of the first two volumes of CWG, as well as *Friendship With God*. I confess that I haven't read them in their entirety, but I am familiar enough with them (and indeed have done some meditating about them) to discuss them. First off, it may surprise you to learn that I absolutely love about 85% of each of the books! Much of what Mr. Walsch and "God" talk about is awesome! In fact, and here's what may surprise you the most, the great majority of the stuff in those books is equal to early Christian teachings which have, in great measure, been muddied over and "religionized" over the centuries. Indeed, Mr. Walsch uses uniquely biblical phrases and sayings time upon time upon time in his books. If you read the Bible, and especially the New Testament, for yourself you'll see exactly what I'm talking about. I think if any of the disciples were around today to write a book about the things Jesus taught it would sound a lot like CWG/FWG. I have been so frustrated at my inability to get across the true Christian definition of hell, but when I went back to reread some of CWG's description of it I thought to myself, "This is so close to what I've been trying to say all along!" Not exactly, but very close. So go read how he describes "God's" view of hell and then reread my letters on the subject with that framework in mind (if you still have them, that is) and hopefully you'll better understand what I'm trying to communicate.

I also really like the lesson that Life is not about learning but *re*-learning stuff we have forgotten. Just a few days ago I was remembering back to my childhood and thinking about how pure and innocent, how loving and absolutely trusting my relationship with God was, as opposed to my adult, sophisticated, and "maturer" understanding of the ways of the spirit. It's true, there are many things I understand now that I'm older that I couldn't as a child, but the purity and totality of trust gets lost with age, as we learn to depend more and more on ourselves and think we can handle everything. Hah, what a laugh! I know that Mr. Walsch was talking about something more esoteric than this, but hey, I apply it as I see fit. =)

I do, however, have two major concerns with his works. I know that they aren't gospel to you, so you don't really need to defend them or anything, but here are my thoughts. The first thing that bugs me about CWG is what bugs me about almost every single New Age book in existence. They all <u>love</u> to use Jesus as a great Teacher/Master and quote ad infinitum his "warm fuzzy" sayings. But these same people <u>completely ignore</u> the so-called "hard sayings" of Jesus! I've never read one New Age book that mentions the fact that Jesus talked more about hell than anyone else in the entire Bible. I've never come across the parable of the sheep and the goats in a New Age book. I've never heard about Jesus uttering the phrase "where there will be weeping and gnashing of teeth", although he said it many a time. Yes, Jesus said many wonderful things that warm the heart and bring us closer to God, but he also talked of hell's existence and God's righteous anger, which I believe can also bring one closer to God. Now, as I've said before, it's true that many Christians have misunderstood and/or mistaught his reasons for warning people about judgment. Or maybe to be more precise I should say that many preachers have taught this idea with insensitivity, and in a way that turns off nonbelievers. In any event, this is the reason why there is such a strong stereotype of the biblical hell out there.

Back to my main point, though. Jesus is so much more than the detached, ethereal "mystic" that New Age authors and speakers seem to want to portray him as. To reduce him simply to an Eastern sage who was ahead of his time and walked around saying weird but wonderful things is like saying Hamlet was simply wishy-washy and couldn't make up his mind. Not only did Jesus utter the most profound and heartwarming things ever said by man (and woman, which should be implied), but he also talked about a future judgment day and the very real possibility of being separated from God forever. But he's even more than that, too! If we only look at Jesus' theological teachings we get only a one or two-dimensional view of him, and miss out on perhaps the most important thing about him, the thing that allows us to relate to him and take what he said seriously. He was a *real* person! He lived not on some isolated mountaintop dropping pearls of wisdom to the unwashed masses below, but descended right into the muck and mire of our world, with all its dirt, corruption, rage, and evil (yes, evil), and showed *real* people living in the *real* world a way to be friends and children of God—a way that doesn't require glassy-eyed mysticism, mechanical obedience, arcane knowledge or anything else but trust and simple faith in him, bound in truth and love.
Here's the second, and even more troubling, point—at least to me. Neal has God implying that Hitler was not really a monster from His point of view because death is, in actuality, the greatest thing that could happen to a person. In another part of his book he and "God" converse about not judging other people's paradigms, and advises against holding up signs saying "We're right/We have the truth: but should instead

hold up signs that say "Ours is Just Another Way." When you couple these notions to each other, you get something that must be regarded by any decent person as utterly horrifying. If we are to consistently apply Neal's principles, then we are forced to regard Hitler's 'final solution' as Just Another Way. Do we really believe this??!? Were the Allies nothing more than a consortium of nations who had a different version of what was good, and happened to win? It's true that in Hitler's mind, in his paradigm, he was in the right. Unless he was completely psychotic through and through, he believed that what he was doing was for the good of the world, or at least the good of his country and himself. But does Neal Donald Walsch truly believe that the mass extermination of millions of people simply because they weren't blond-haired and blue-eyed is Just Another Way?!? Just another paradigm that happens to be different from ours? How can anyone with an ounce of intelligence and compassion go along with this notion? But wait, it gets even worse! According to Neal's God, death, no matter the manner in which it comes, is truly the greatest thing that can happen to a human. If this is true, then Hitler is not merely not a monster, but he is in truth one of the noblest men ever to have lived, for he sent *millions upon millions* to their eternal happiness! Under this paradigm, a mass murderer, a serial killer, and a suicide victim are all some of the most noble, most virtuous people there are! Imagine a man, a psychotic man, who believes that in order to please God he must kidnap a newborn baby, impale it on a poker, stick it in a lit fireplace and slowly dismember it with forceps, all while the mother is forced to watch. My god! I feel physically ill just writing such a sentence—doesn't your stomach threaten to empty its contents as you try to imagine such an act? Just Another Way?!? I'm sorry, but to me there *are* certain paradigms that should be judged, and judged most harshly. You may say that this is an extreme example that no one could truly believe. Well, with all the wackos out there in the world, I'm not so sure. But even were I to agree with that notion, the fact remains that it is theoretically possible to believe such a thing, and under the CWG worldview, that person or group can legitimately claim to be just one more way to God. And besides, this baby-killing cult is merely hastening the newborn's journey to paradise, so they're actually doing good! As Casca says in Julius Caesar, "He that cuts off twenty years of life cuts off so many years of fearing death." You see, Jordan (and perhaps you agree), the problem with much of this mushy Don't Judge Anybody talk is that it sounds good, but in order to apply it consistently, and not just when it gives you warm fuzzies, you are forced to assent to unimpeachably foul ideas.

This is what appeals to me so much about Christianity. Not only can the biblical paradigm be supported by science, history, and archaeology, but it is absolutely self-consistent in its world-view! If you take any

Christian principle and apply it to any relevant idea's logical extreme, it still makes sense and satisfies the soul, quite unlike Neal Donald Walsch's worldview. Christianity easily describes an amazing God who is Love unbounded, as well as a God who experiences anger; the Christian worldview has no trouble at all describing mankind as possessing bright and shining souls while at the same time being marred by depravity and sin. This is made even more astounding by the fact that Christianity was not expounded by one man, like a Joseph Smith who found some divine plates of gold all by himself, or a Mohammed who happened to walk into a cave and come out with the "Word of God" all by himself, but was revealed by forty different people over a period of several thousand years, and still is completely consistent with itself! That alone is a mind-blower and reason to seriously consider Christianity as, at the very least, a superior worldview. You're absolutely right, believing you're right and others are less right is dangerous, and in the wrong hands, leads to much suffering. But so does the other way. For in not judging at all we leave ourselves impotent in the face of blatant and monstrous evil.

The other thing that bothers me about taking Hitler's actions so lightly is that it reduces our life here on earth to meaninglessness. This is one point where Mr. Walsch's views just don't jibe with each other. On the one hand, the purpose of life here on earth is to re-learn that we are All There Is, that we are God. On the other hand, killing someone is in actuality a good because it sends us to eternal bliss, where we will fully understand that we are All There Is, that we are God. Huh? Why not just all take our own lives now, end this illusion, and travel to someplace eternally happy and peaceful and good? Why do we need to re-learn who we are if we're going to find out anyway as soon as we die? What's the point? Why bother trying to curb violence and death, why bother helping out people less fortunate than us, why bother doing anything at all if when we die nothing we did here matters? This aspect of his paradigm makes no sense in the real world.

As I said at the beginning, I was greatly blessed by the majority of the stuff I read in his books. It's just that these two issues in particular (call them the Jesus problem and the Hitler problem, if you will) jump out at me with undeniable clarity and I am therefore unable to believe that Neal's conversations with "God" are 100% genuine, and unable to take what is said in his books as "gospel".

But, as Dennis Miller (I think) says, maybe it's just me. ;)

Peace,
Jeremy

Sent: Tuesday, August 28, 2001
Subject: Re: Conversations...

Very Nice!

I'm off to work now, but anticipate digesting your thoughtful missive tonight!
Jai bhagwan!...........(hee-hee)

From: Jordan Adams <jadams@_____.net>
To: Jeremy Seely <jeremy_seely@_____.com>
Sent: Monday, October 8, 2001
Subject: feelings on 9/11

Hey Brother Jeres,

I've had a few thoughts and I thought I'd share them. Seems like the fanatical Muslims are feeling pretty sure these days that they have the pipeline to God's ear.
Seems we don't quite "get it". Oh we're good people and we're trying hard, but in the end we're Christians so we don't know the *true* Savior, so we're screwed. The Muslims have the key and if you don't believe them just check out their book. They have the Holy Book and it's Gospel. If we don't follow it we're less than them – in fact we're infidels. Because they have the secret, and God's ear, they have the right to impose their way on us. They have the right to preach and convert us because after all, we don't understand how ignorant we are. I could go on and on but I think you get the point.

I couldn't be more sure that the whole thing is a crock. We insult God to the nth degree when we try to cram him into one of our tiny little religions. To make matters worse, we then have "Holy Wars" in his name. Whether it's the Christian slaughter of the Muslims in the Crusades of not too long ago or the events of 9/11, it's abundantly clear that we need a new way of looking at God. A way that doesn't claim mastery of his words. A way that doesn't claim a monopoly of his ear. A way that once and for all does away with dogma. Take all these books, these "holy books" that seem to cause so much trouble and conflict and burn them. Yes burn them. Burn them in God's name and beg for his forgiveness for making him so small.

I know it feels good inside to say "God bless America". I love saying it myself. But the truth is God doesn't bless America. God doesn't even see

America, and we certainly can't claim providence to him as a Country. God sees his beautiful planet. He doesn't see boundaries, countries, or religions. He just sees us slaughtering each other in his name. So I challenge you Jeres to see an expanded version of God. Go bigger and better than your book. Think bigger. Think past books. Think more loving than the linear good/bad paradigm. Think smarter than the tired punishment paradox. Go past the human projection.

I'll leave you with this letter from God:

Sunday October 07, 2001

This Just In:
JUDAISM, CHRISTIANITY
AND ISLAM ABOLISHED
By God!

I hereby abolish Judaism, Christianity, and Islam. They have caused Me nothing but trouble since their inception. I acknowledge that they were a mistake right from the start. But those were dark times indeed and I could see no other way to discipline those unruly squabbling siblings.

As of this moment, Judaism, Christianity, and Islam have been declared obsolete and irrelevant. They have absolutely no currency in the overall scheme of cosmic evolution. As for the other belief systems, I shall be reviewing them soon and if they are found no longer useful, they too will simply vanish from the face of the Earth. Which bright aspect of Myself was it who said: "Monotheism breeds fanatical anthropocentrism, which eventually destroys Earth"?
Let no more be said about the Matter.

Please do not EVER AGAIN commit atrocities in MY name. I am an Extremely Eclectic Entity with a Multitude of Attributes and Personalities and each one of you is indeed a direct and true manifestation of Myself.

Monotheists, kindly wise up to the fact that I may ultimately be One Being, but I am certainly not in favor of being worshipped as such. Worship means service, and the best service you can perform is to yourself, your communities, and to all living creatures large and small.

You will NOT be hearing from ME again. It's too much work trying to communicate through linear language.
Be Well and Happy and Continue to Evolve and Mature as a Species.

WHO'S GOT GOD?

YAHWEH/GOD/ALLAH

Great Spirit

Source

The One

Etc.

☙❧

Sent: Monday, October 8, 2001
Subject: Re: feelings on 9/11

Hey God,

Great idea! D'ya mind if I make a suggestion, though? Before we abolish religion, let's abolish all the governments of Earth first. They have been responsible for human slaughter many multiple orders of magnitude greater than anything religion ever has. Life will be utopia once we get rid of these twin menaces.

Your faithful servant.

P.S. While not excusing the many evils committed by both sides during the Crusades, it is useful to remember that they were touched off when fanatic Muslims—the Seljuk Turks—invaded Jerusalem, threw out the peaceful Muslims, who enjoyed peace with the Christians, and started persecuting the Christians, along with just about everybody else. You're God, though, so of course you already knew that.

Sent: Tuesday, October 9, 2001
Subject: Re: feelings on 9/11

Hey Very Nice,

I am chuckling as I write this due to your clever reply. I do feel the essence of my suggestion was not addressed however.
The fanaticism to which you correctly refer is caused by a claiming of the ear and motivations of God. A monopoly if you will, of his desires. Our book is the real word not yours. Do you see the base insanity here? Do you see the endless conflict and bloodshed which will result by trying to cram the Infinite or Uncrammable into one religion? My suggestion that

God is bigger than Christianity, Judaism, and Islam combined, was not addressed.

Love and Blessings,
J

☯︎

Sent: Monday, October 15, 2001
Subject: The essence of your suggestion.
Jordan,

Sorry I didn't address your main concern in my last little "letter to God". You know what, though, I've been dealing with that, either directly or indirectly, in just about every single letter I've written to you over the past year. Many a time I have agreed with you that yes, God is bigger than any mere religion, and that yes, believing you have THE truth can be a very dangerous thing, and yes, in many times and many places throughout history, that belief has led to horrible acts of violence IN THE NAME OF GOD, and that yes, God has nothing to do with it and is immensely saddened (and angered) by it. I also know that at one point, I talked briefly about the flipside of this: all the good that has been done IN THE NAME OF GOD. Because of religion, we today have the benefit of education and medicine. Democracy and civil rights. The abolition of slavery. Science. Mercy. Charity. Faith. Hope. Love. And on and on and on. Would you rather we live without any one of those things? Well, they came about as a direct result of people believing that they could know God. My main point in my last letter was that if you really truly believe that we need to get rid of the religions "of the book," as it were, you should also be in favor of dismantling all the governments of the world and living in anarchy. The correlation is EXACTLY the same. When the few have power over the many, whether it be voluntary as with democracy or involuntary as with monarchy, totalitarianism, etc., there exists the possibility to perform acts of great good or great evil. THERE IS ALWAYS THE CHOICE. What you're saying in your letters is that, since a structured belief in God begets the possibility that someone might think God exults in having them plow airplanes into occupied buildings, we should get rid of it altogether! By the same token, since there is the possibility of evil arising out of structured government, we should similarly get rid of it altogether. And really, when you look at it, you should be putting religion on the backburner. Man's inhumanity to man because of government and a nonbelief in God, or a spurning of God, is so much larger as to make the Crusades look like child's play. When you think of how many people were killed and forced to live in misery as a result of just three men who had governmental power--Hitler, Stalin, and Mao-Tse Tung, it should make you forget completely about what has been done in religion's name. And that's just three guys! And hey, come to think of it, there is the possibility of evil being done by doctors and teachers, too. Let's get rid of 'em! Hmm, I think you begin to see my point...

What you're really saying deep down, Jordan, is that you're anti-choice. You may not realize it, and you may not even agree with it when it comes out in the open, but you don't want humans to have the choice to choose between good and evil. You would rather have us all be robots that don't believe in anything except everything, and once everyone believes in nothing/everything, there will be no evil, only love. Do you truly believe this? Do you really think that if we got rid of all specific beliefs in God there would be utopia on this planet? Do you really believe that we have been evolving upward as human beings, and will soon reach a point where we will all vibrate together and reach a new plane of spiritual existence? I don't think so. Were you around for the twentieth century?!? There was more slaughter worldwide in that hundred years than in all of the rest of history combined! No matter how one tries to deny it, the sinfulness of mankind has not changed one iota since the very first man and woman walked this planet. It is inescapable. But so is the beauty and wonder. My point is, don't look at only one side of the equation.

I frankly find it offensive and somewhat disturbing and depressing that you can, in your mind, equate the actions and beliefs of a few thousand, perhaps even a few million, evil people with the BILLIONS of believers worldwide who worship God, as they see Him, in peace and love. And because of the few rotten apples in the barrel, you honestly have come to the conclusion that we should get rid of the whole thing altogether. When you place the good done in the name of God next to the evil done in the name of God, I think you'll see the scales tipping WAY over onto the good side, Jordan. It is true that, as someone once said, religious feelings make possible the worst acts of cruelty, but they also make possible the highest acts of Good. This is because our religious feelings touch us deeper in our soul and drive us to action more than any other kind of feeling, for as it is said, what a person believes about God shapes his entire character. Every action and point of being about a person is derived from what he or she believes about God. When it comes to God, Jordan, the stakes are incredibly, infinitely high. But that is what makes "the game" so important to play.

You know, I can argue all I want about all the logical reasons why one should believe in Jesus and the Bible. All that can do, though, is open someone's mind. It can't carry them across the threshold into true, joyous belief. In the end, what we must rely upon is our own personal experience and how we interpret it. That is what makes this whole business of God so important. We continually have a choice as to how we respond to our experiences, and the choices we make have consequences in our lives! We can use and take into our beings the Light that God gives of Himself, or we can reject it, ignore it, and cover it up. As human beings we are each constantly moving in one direction or the other. I have tried as best I can to make the overarching principle of my life (which basically means I take two steps forward, one step back) one of moving closer to the Light and embracing it.

You said you couldn't be more sure that the whole thing was a crock. Well, I couldn't be more sure that it's not, because of the experiences I've had in my life as a result of making this choice, day by day (and also because of the experiences I've had when I do not make the choice). One day when I was about eighteen or nineteen, I was feeling adrift at sea with my life. I was going through one of the many crises, as we all do, of "What am I going to do with my life?" I had just rediscovered God and knew that there was something (or some things) He had created me for and put me here to do. But at this particular moment in my life I had absolutely no idea what it was, and I was in a deep depression (as I am wont to do) over it. As I sat on the couchbed in the room I was using while staying at my mom's house (this was during a holiday time and the dorms were closed) I closed my eyes and began to pray and ask God for help. I imagined a box, suspended and slowly spinning, inside my chest. Inside that box, I asked God to place what it was He wanted from me. I told Him I was going to count to three and open the box. I slowly started counting in my head, imagining this spinning, floating box, and part of me thought to myself "This is so lame. What are you doing? You expect God to jump out of this imaginary box and tell you What To Do With Your Life? Sigh." But I ignored the voice and went on counting anyway. As I got to three and opened the box in my mind, something happened to me totally unexpected and without my bidding or unconscious psychological projection. The box melted away and three words flew confidently and boldly out—big, bold, glowing words all in caps. Three words that literally changed my life. They were:

SEARCH FOR ME

I cannot describe how I knew this, but I knew-that-I-knew that these words had come from Outside me. They completely surprised me—floored me even—and hot tears of what, I don't know—thankfulness, awe, inspiration, something!—poured down my cheeks. It was the first spiritual experience I had ever had, and still the most intense. It continues to guide me to this day. Since that time, I have become convinced that the One who gave me those words was the God who is described—not totally explained, but described and revealed—in the Bible and by Jesus. As I have drawn closer to this God, I have seen and experienced many wonderful things. I have been instantaneously healed of a physical affliction (no, not at some ridiculous faith-healing convention but in the privacy of my bedroom) which has never recurred to this day, I have received specific and real answers to prayer (stuff like the exact amount of money I desperately needed arriving at my doorstep totally unexpected by me, or struggling mightily with a specific issue or doubt or depression only to have my pastor speak a message on that exact subject the next day, etc.), I have seen others be blessed in the same way, and most important I have been given (and I use the words 'been given' very deliberately) a sense of peace, purpose, and "blessed assurance" in the reality, the actual nuts-and-bolts reality, of this God I have been striving to draw near to.

This is not to say I have become a saint since that day. Far from it. Since then, I have done some horrible deeds, thought some ugly thoughts. And I don't say that in a romantic sense, as if to put myself on a higher pedestal by showing how humble I am. There are some truly evil things about me, some disgustingly black corners of my soul. I am a sinner, in the fullest and nastiest and messiest sense of the word. I think if you're honest about yourself, Jordan, you too would agree with this about your own life. But this also confirms my belief in the God I worship and love! Because the depths of ugliness I surprise myself with…he's already told me about in the Bible. He already knew it! And I have also experienced the incredible grace and completely unmerited forgiveness that He offers, and that I read about in the Bible. I've said this so many times in my conversations with God: "God, I don't know how or why you do it. If I were you and saw me acting and thinking the way I do, I would have vaporized me in a flash of totally justified anger LONG ago! WHY in the world do you love me?!?" Knowing the ugly part of my self, and knowing that God loves me anyway, never tires of forgiving me and always ecstatically welcomes me back into His presence, knowing that He even DIED for me…while I was rejecting Him!…, makes me literally fall on my knees in humble gratitude and unexclaimable adoration. Paul's letter to the Romans (5:7-8): "Very rarely will anyone die for a righteous man, though for a good man someone might possibly dare to die. But God demonstrates his own love for us in this: While we were still sinners, Christ died for us!" To this I can only be speechless.

Shalom,

Jeremy

P.S. How could I write and not mention the terrible tragedy that befell our nation? It's a month old now, so pretty much everything that can be said about how awful it was has been said. Just the other night I went back and watched the hours of news I recorded that day, in order that I might not become numbed by hearing about it every day, and hearing it being described as nothing more than "the incident." Seeing how our nation has come together and been unafraid to show love for this country again, seeing how many people are really looking at what is of true importance in their lives, seeing people use the word God and not look over their shoulder in fear of the ACLU Lawsuit Brigade has been a tremendous hope for me. It's vindicated my faith in the strong foundation this country is built on. This country is FAR from perfect, but it truly is the best country ever created in the history of mankind. Most of us just forgot that for awhile. In the Genesis story of Joseph (i.e. the Technicolor Dreamcoat guy), Joseph is sold into slavery by his brothers. Many years later the story comes full circle as Joseph has risen in the ranks to become the second most powerful man in all of Egypt and is in a position to save the lives of his brothers and the rest of his family when they come to Egypt in a desperate search for food. After his father dies his brothers become afraid that Joseph will take revenge on them but instead he says this: "You meant evil against me, but God meant it for good." I believe we can apply this in some measure to what happened on September 11. Certainly this was an evil act, an act where evil stripped off its masks and showed its true face...but God. Once again, that awesome phrase! Not only is this a time in which we see evil unmasked, we also get to fall down in awe at seeing the Master Weaver at work. God can take anything...anything!...and weave it into His tapestry of goodness and love. In the face of this despicable violence we hear about the multitude of goodness that has spilled out of the hearts of people across the entire globe. When we finally get to see the finished work we will know, with the hindsight of eternity, that although there were terrible evils that happened and heartbreaking suffering endured, these black threads come together in such a perfect, artistic way as to complete the rest of the tapestry and make the bright parts even brighter. And this is what I choose to dwell on.

Sent: Monday, October 15, 2001
Subject: Addendum

I had another thought about what I wrote. In my defense of religion, I hope you didn't get the idea that I myself am into religion. I think you know by now that I am not a religious guy. Spiritual yes, but not too religious, and yes there is a big difference. I personally don't care too much for big 'R' Religion. Religion is all man-made. Religion takes the things of the spirit, codifies them, sets up the three 'R's: Rules, Regulations, and Rituals, and puts God into a box, saying "This is God in here, and nowhere else!" Exactly like you say all the time.

But, and this is my point, it's not all bad. Like I said, religion is directly responsible for most of everything that is good in this world. When it gets dangerous is when it starts to do the things I mentioned above. Rituals are great things as long as you keep the spirit behind it intact. Often, though, ritual becomes empty and meaningless, sort of a "doing your duty for God" kind of thing. Rules and regulations are good things, too, as long as they don't run amok and become an end in and of themselves. This leads to the belief that having the right answers about God is more important than *knowing* God.

I hope you can see that the Bible is not a religion. Religions have sprung up around it, yes, and many of these religions I agree with a whole lot of what they believe in. But the Bible itself, and Jesus Himself, are not religions. They are bigger than that. The Bible, essentially, is a record of God's working in human history, which culminates in Jesus and his message, his gospel. That's it, and nothing more. But if you believe what the Bible says about Jesus, you realize that he is not just one among many--he is unique and stands above all others. Mohammed, Moses, Gandhi, Buddha, and all the others brought many different facets of Light into the world and much of what each of them say is worthy of study and application, but none of them are worthy of being worshipped but Jesus. And none of them deserve to be shoved into a box and labeled as Religion. I know that you agree. I *have* expanded past the religion paradigm, many other believers in Jesus have as well, and I hope you can too, in the way you view the 'Christian' faith.

Just because we can't know *everything* about God doesn't mean we can't know anything.

Especially if God chooses to show us.
Jeremy

P.S. I just saw a new book yesterday that I know you would really dig. It's written by Philip Yancey, who is just incredible--you would appreciate him very much. His new book is called <u>Soul Survivor</u>, and it's subtitled "How My Faith Survived the Church". I skimmed through it, and it was just awesome! I kept thinking yes! yes! to myself as I read it. I think you would find him very sympathetic to your misgivings about religion.

Sent: Monday, October 22, 2001
Subject: Re: The essence of your suggestion.

Hey Jeres,

Thank you for reminding me that yes there are many more good things done in the name of religion than bad. It is always good to be brought back to a state of balance by sharing ideas, getting feedback, and adjusting accordingly. I know I'm prone to bellicose and sweeping statements! I whole-heartedly agree with huge parts of your last letter. I found it well-ordered and thoughtful.

Some disagreements,
You said:

> *When you think of how many people were killed and forced to live in misery as a result of just three men who had governmental power— Hitler, Stalin, and Mao-Tse Tung, it should make you forget completely about what has been done in religion's name.*

This is that same kind of logic a child employs when he's caught with his hand in the cookie jar. He says but Mom! Joey ate 3 cookies so it's ok that I'm only eating two!
If the Crusades took "only" 2 million lives trying to get people to talk to God through Jesus instead of Mohammed, and Hitler, Stalin, and Mao-Tse Tung took 20 million, I should *forget completely* about the 2 million killed in religion's name? Jeremy, fascism is fascism.

You said:

> *What you're really saying deep down, Jordan, is that you're anti-choice. You may not realize it, and you may not even agree with it when it comes out in the open, but you don't want humans to have the choice to choose between good and evil. You would rather have us all be robots that don't believe in anything except everything, and once everyone believes in nothing/everything, there will be no evil, only love. Do you truly believe this? Do you really think that if we got rid of all specific beliefs in God there would be utopia on this planet? Do you really believe that we have been evolving upward as human beings, and will soon reach a point where we will all vibrate together and reach a new plane of spiritual existence? I don't think so. Were you around for the twentieth century?!? There was more slaughter worldwide in that hundred years than in all of the rest of history combined! No matter how one tries to deny it, the sinfulness of mankind has not changed one iota since the very first man and woman walked this*

planet. It is inescapable. But so is the beauty and wonder. My point is, don't look at only one side of the equation.

This couldn't be further from the truth. I am *exactly* asking you to choose. I am asking you to choose between good and evil....I believe that it's a form of evil to – with our limited minds – try to squish God down into one little religion, or one little way of thinking about him. I believe it's a form of evil to ignore all the evidence in the last 4 billion years – not just 2 thousand – that God is alive and well and talks to us in many ways. I believe it's a form of evil and *violence* to petrify people with a threat of eternal scorching – in God's name none the less! Talk about evil!
So yes, I am asking you to have faith Jeremy. Have faith that God is way bigger than what a bunch of Monks wrote about him a couple of thousand years ago. Have faith that God is weeping right now. He's weeping because people who claim a monopoly on his ears and intentions are killing in his name. I say it again: God is bigger and better than just one path. You always do a great job at describing God's love and availability to us all. Believe me, he's just as available to a Buddhist prayer as he is to a Christian one. As always I don't ask you to take my word for it. I always encourage you to pray and get your own answers. Ask God directly and earnestly how big he is.

ಬಂಡ

Sent: Tuesday, October 23, 2001
Subject: Re: The essence of your suggestion

Hi Jeres,

Hope you got my last communiqué. I am concerned as always, that you know how deeply I want you to know, that I don't want you to feel I undervalue your beliefs in any way. At one point you said you were offended. Please know that my love for you supercedes **any and all needs** that I have for you to come to understand how God reveals himself to me. You either will come to understand it or you won't, it will not affect my feelings for you. There are some Buddhist principles regarding being offended that I'll share with you if you are so inclined :-)
If I did offend you I am sorry Dear Brother, it was not my intention.

I am deeply moved by your testimony and am honored you chose to share it with me. When my eyes aren't bloodshot I'm going to share some of my testimony with you as well. When I do, it may surprise you to know that I pray to Jesus too. We do have differences on how many Saviors there are, and on the amount of paths to God, but I think we're in agreement that Jesus had a main line to the Big Guy. He laid it out for us – eternity, love, non-judgment, forgiveness, simply awesome to the nth degree. He "got it"

As always,
Love and Blessings
El Jordano

୧୦୧୪

From: Jeremy Seely <jeremy_seely@_____.com>
To: Jordan Adams <jadams@_____.net>
Sent: Tuesday, April 2, 2002
Subject: No Religion for Easter

Dear Jordan,

Just a heads-up—I'm sending you a short article in the mail that was written by my pastor. It's called "Why Religion Doesn't Work For Me This Easter," and I think there's a bunch of stuff in there you'll resonate with. It's about how religion doesn't have the answers that we need; only following the person of Jesus does.

Blessings,

Jeres

Sent: Saturday, April 6, 2002
Subject: Re: No Religion for Easter

Hey Jeres,

Thanks for the great article you sent me from your Pastor. I liked him when I heard his sermon and I still like him after I read his letter "Why Religion Doesn't Work For Me This Easter."

I especially like the part about religious man made "add-ons." I agree whole heartedly that man made add-ons and dogma only serve to weaken our relationship with God and divert us from the power available to us but for the mere asking.

For me personally, the more I deepen my relationship with God, the more I simply don't care about any religion at all. Interestingly enough, my need to have people see (and validate) my way of talking to God has greatly dissipated also. Almost as if God has washed me clean in a bath of understanding and peace. There were points in the Pastor's letter that I simply didn't agree with, albeit small ones – I nonetheless wanted to say "yeah but"... but then I realized I didn't care so much. Not didn't care in the sense of not caring literally, but more of a releasing. He's clearly "plugged in" and to me, that's Divine. It's not for me to question. Conversely, it has simultaneously taken the need for me to defend my way of talking to God away. God has taken it away. Ahhhhhhhhh. I may now stand defenseless.

We still have the same "differences" Jeres, but oh boy, am I lucky to know you. For through my knowing you, I have come to understand God and his ways that much more. I realize that I have in many ways, more in common with you than some of my angrier Buddhist and Interfaith friends. There's something beautiful and illuminating about standing up for your truths and at the same time loving someone else's truths – fully.
Keep deepening that beautiful relationship you have. Keep asking and affirming more revelation be given on to you. You know you'll get it

Deep Love,
El Jordano

൞

Sent: Sunday, April 7, 2002
Subject: Our "Differences"

Wow. You know, one may look at all our letters and think "Why bother? Why do these guys spend so much time articulating what they personally believe, trying to persuade the other? Why do they spend so much time talking about their disagreements? Can't they just have fun together?" Heh heh. That's actually a pretty good point, as I've thought that a few times myself. I think this extended conversation has been extremely valuable, though, don't you? After all, one's ideas are important. Ideas lead to actions in the real world, and perhaps even to eternal destinies, so it is vital for people to contemplate and discuss them. I think the quest for truth is one of the most important and noble undertakings a human can attempt. I am privileged and honored (and opened and educated) any time I enter discussion of eternal and divine truths, much more so when it reaches the depths that ours has. And of course we did have fun together when we were performing the show. Which isn't to say that these emails haven't been fun—they have! I think our dialogue has been the epitome of 'disagreeing without being disagreeable', as well as a great example of different people finding common ground and celebrating that. It has been the very definition of Tolerance. <u>It has been well worth it.</u>

Peace and Blessings,

Jeremy

From: Jeremy Seely <jeremy_seely@_____.com>
and Jordan Adams <jadams@_____.net>
To: You dear reader
Sent: Today
Subject: Epilogue

Dear Reader,

Well, that's it. This is the end of our correspondence. You may ask yourself, 'Where's the rest of it? Where's the satisfying conclusion?' Well, being that we never set out with the intention of turning these letters into anything, the conversation just kind of petered out. Real life intruded. Jeremy married Monica and went to graduate school, Jordan moved to Florida, started a successful career in sports announcing and also got married, and the kind of free time we once had to spend hours upon hours composing emails evaporated as a new season of life started for each of us. In the end, pretty much everything of value had been said anyway.

The question in the book's title remains unanswered as well: Who's got God? This is by design, for we believe that this is the wrong question to ask. To ask it (or to answer it) shows a fundamental misunderstanding of the ways of the spirit. To say 'I've got God,' or 'God is on our team,' 'God is with our political party,' 'God is with our denomination or religion' is to get the whole enchilada all wrong. In anything, you must always ask not whether God is on your team, but whether *you* are on *God's* team. God owns the team, not you. Do not ask, 'Who's got God?' but ask instead, 'Who does *God* have?' And if you really want to get specific and ask a question that actually *means* something, ask:

Does God have Me?

And so this brings us to the close. We may have left the original question of the book unanswered, but there is still a fitting conclusion to be had. We believe it lies in the closing words of the last letter written between the two, and so they will be reprinted below:

> *One may look at all our letters and think 'Why bother? Why do these guys spend so much time articulating what they personally believe, trying to persuade the other? Why do they spend so much time talking about their disagreements? Can't they just have fun together?' Heh heh. That's actually a pretty good point, as I've thought that a few times myself. I think this extended conversation has been extremely valuable, though, don't you? After all, one's ideas are important. Ideas lead to actions in the real world, and perhaps even to eternal destinies, so it is vital for people to contemplate and discuss them. I think the quest for truth is one of the most important and noble undertakings a human can attempt. I am privileged and honored (and opened and educated) any time I enter discussion of eternal and divine truths, much more so when it reaches the depths that ours has. Which isn't to say that these emails haven't been fun—they have! I think our dialogue has been the epitome of 'disagreeing without being disagreeable', as well as a great example of different people finding common ground and celebrating that. It has been the very definition of Tolerance. It has been well worth it.*

Indeed it has been worth it. And if any of our readers have picked up even one valuable thing from these letters, whether it be a newfound spiritual awakening, a respect for other beliefs, even a bolstering of their own faith, then that value has been increased a hundred-fold.

Blessings
Shalom
Namaste
Peace

GOD BLESS YOU
Jeres & El Jordano

REFERENCES

[1] Lewis, C.S. *Mere Christianity*.
[2] Lewis, C.S. *The Great Divorce*.
[3] Collett, Sidney. *All About the Bible*. Old Tappan, N.J.: Fleming H. Revell, n.d. p.314-315
[4] Green, William Henry. *General Introduction to the Old Testament - The Text*. New York: Charles Scribner's sons, 1899. p.81
[5] Ramsay, W.M. *St. Paul the Traveller and the Roman Citizen*. Grand Rapids: Baker Book House, 1962. p.222
[6] Stoner, Peter W. *Science Speaks*. Chicago: Moody Press, 1963. pp. 100-105
[7] Shelley, Bruce L. *Church History in Plain Language*. Dallas: Word Publishing, 1995. pp. 206, 211, 192
[8] Kreeft, Peter and Tacelli, Ronald K. *Handbook of Christian Apologetics*. Downers Grove: InterVarsity Press, 1994. p. 304
[9] Carson, D.A. quoted in Strobel, Lee. *The Case For Christ*. Grand Rapids: ZondervanPublishingHouse, 1998. p.165
[10] Lewis, C.S. *The Great Divorce*.
[11] Eldridge, Niles. *Reinventing Darwin: The Great Debate at the High Table of Evolutionary Theory*. New York: John Wiley and Sons, 1995. p.95
[12] Letter from Charles Darwin to W. Graham, 3 July 1881, *Life and Letters of Charles Darwin*, vol. 1, 316, cited in Hanegraaff, Hank, The Face That Demonstrates the Farce of Evolution, Nashville: Word Publishing, 1998. p.24-25
[13] Darwin, Charles. *The Descent of Man*. Chap. VI "On the Affinities and Genealogy of Man," sect. "On the Birthplace and Antiquity of Man." cited in Hanegraaff, Hank, *The Face That Demonstrates the Farce of Evolution*, Nashville: Word Publishing, 1998. p.25
[14] Huxley, Thomas H. *Lay Sermons, Addresses and Reviews*. New York: Appleton, 1871. p. 20. cited in Hanegraaff, Hank, *The Face That Demonstrates the Farce of Evolution*, Nashville: Word Publishing, 1998. p.25
[15] Vision Statement, *ReCreation Foundation*, www.cwg.org
[16] California Proposition 22. Also known as the Defense of Marriage Act, it was a proposition passed by 61% of California voters in 2000 to amend state law to define marriage as a union between a man and a woman. It's author was State Senator William "Pete" Knight.
[17] Walsch, Neale Donald. *Conversations With God: An Uncommon Dialog, Book 2*. Charlottesville: Hampton Roads Publishing Company, Inc., 1997. pp. 31-35
[18] Walsch, Neale Donald. *Conversations With God: An Uncommon Dialog, Book 2*. Charlottesville: Hampton Roads Publishing Company, Inc., 1997. pp. 36-40

FURTHER READING

Jeremy

Anything by C.S. Lewis and Philip Yancey, but especially:

The Jesus I Never Knew by Philip Yancey

Mere Christianity by C.S. Lewis

When Bad Christians Happen To Good People by Dave Burchett

Soul Survivor: How My Faith Survived the Church by Philip Yancey

Velvet Elvis by Rob Bell

The Ragamuffin Gospel by Brennan Manning

Mything Out On Jesus and His Teachings by Tim Timmons

The Case For Christ and *The Case For Faith* by Lee Strobel

Handbook of Christian Apologetics by Peter Kreeft and Ronald K. Tacellii

Evidence That Demands a Verdict and *More Than A Carpenter* by Josh McDowell

The Podcasts from Mars Hill Bible Church, Pastor Rob Bell

Jordan

The Power of Now and *New Earth* by Eckhart Tolle

Loving What Is by Byron Katie

Thank God for Evolution by Michael Dowd

Peaceful Warrior and *Body Mind Mastery* by Dan Millman

Power vs. Force by David Hawkins

Fearless and *Mind Shift* by Stephen Chandler

Conversations with God by Neal Donald Walsch

A Course in Miracles by Marianne Williamson

ABOUT THE AUTHORS

Jeremy Seely holds an M.A. in Educational Psychology from Chapman University. He worked for 13 years in the field of drama therapy, helping abused women and their children, drug addicts, child prostitutes, jailed youth, and others to recover their lives. Currently he lives in California with his wife Monica and son Jacob.

Jeremy also writes as The Skeptical Believer, a blog dedicated to "fearlessly and honestly exploring the challenges of faith in Jesus." Visit him and leave a comment at *www.skbeliever.com*.

Jordan "Jay" Adams holds a Bachelor of Science degree in Communication from Northeastern University. He is co-owner of Fight Zone Television on FOX Sports Network. He lives in Florida with his wife Corinne and baby Hailey McKenzie.

www.ingramcontent.com/pod-product-compliance
Lightning Source LLC
LaVergne TN
LVHW011422080426
835512LV00005B/208